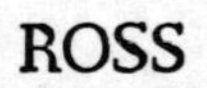
ROSS

ROSS

A Dramatic Portrait by

Terence Rattigan

RANDOM HOUSE:
NEW YORK

Photographs by courtesy of Friedman-Abeles

Manufactured in the United States of America

Dedicated with gratitude to

ANATOLE DE GRUNWALD

who brought Lawrence to me and me to Lawrence

The author gratefully acknowledges his debt to Captain B. H. Liddell Hart, both for the illumination afforded by his book *T. E. Lawrence in Arabia and After* and for his help in checking the script.

Ross *was first presented by David Merrick at the Eugene O'Neill Theatre, New York City, N.Y., on December 26, 1961, with the following cast:*

CAST

(In order of appearance)

FLIGHT LIEUTENANT STOKER	Robert Milli
FLIGHT SERGEANT THOMPSON	Ted Gunther
AIRCRAFTMAN PARSONS	Bill Glover
AIRCRAFTMAN NOLAN	Dennis Cooney
AIRCRAFTMAN DICKINSON	Francis Bethencourt
AIRCRAFTMAN ROSS	John Mills
FRANKS (THE LECTURER)	Kenneth Ruta
GENERAL ALLENBY	John Williams
RONALD STORRS	Anthony Nicholls
COLONEL BARRINGTON	Court Benson
AUDA ABU TAYI	Paul Sparer
THE TURKISH MILITARY GOVERNOR, DERAA DISTRICT	Geoffrey Keen
HAMED	Cal Bellini
RASHID	Joseph Della Sorte
A TURKISH CAPTAIN	Eric Van Nuys
A TURKISH SERGEANT	Thomas Newman
A BRITISH CORPORAL	Del Tenney
A.D.C.	Nicolas Coster
A PHOTOGRAPHER	Scott Graham
SENTRY	John Hallow
FLIGHT LIEUTENANT HIGGINS	James Valentine
GROUP CAPTAIN WOOD	James Craven

Directed by Glen Byam Shaw
Settings and costumes by Motley
Lighting by Al Alloy
Produced by arrangement with H. M. Tennent, Ltd.

The action of the play begins and ends at a Royal Air Force Depot, near London, on an afternoon, the same night and following morning of a day in Winter, 1922. The central passages cover the two years 1916–1918 and are set in the Middle East.

ACT ONE

ACT ONE

Scene one

Scene: An office. Behind a desk sits a FLIGHT LIEUTENANT. *He is an earnest, well-meaning young officer with a manner alternately avuncular and fierce.*

A FLIGHT SERGEANT *stands in front of him. He is an oldish man with a harsh rasping voice that inadequately conceals a soft heart for recruits and a contempt for all officers, including this one.*

FLIGHT LIEUTENANT Next charge.

FLIGHT SERGEANT (*Barking*) Sir. (*He salutes with guardsmanlike punctiliousness, marches to the door, throws it open and shouts gabblingly and with a familiarity born of long usage*) Prisoner and escort, attention, quick march, left right, left right, halt, left turn. Aircraftman Parsons. (PARSONS *is a tough ex-sailor of about thirty-five; of his two escorts,* NOLAN *is young and red-haired, and the other,* DICKINSON, *is an ex-officer of the wartime Army in the ranks of the R.A.F. for economic reasons*)

FLIGHT LIEUTENANT (*Inspecting a charge sheet*) 352179 A.C.2 Parsons?

PARSONS Sir.

FLIGHT LIEUTENANT (*Reading from the charge sheet*) Conduct to the prejudice of good order and Royal Air Force discipline in that on December 16th, 1922, at the 0830-hours color-hoisting parade the accused broke ranks and swore aloud. (*Looking up*) What's all this, Parsons?

PARSONS Slammed my rifle butt on my toe, sir. Lifted my foot half an inch, sir. May have made a slight sound—but only to myself, of course, sir.

FLIGHT LIEUTENANT (*To* FLIGHT SERGEANT) Witness present?

FLIGHT SERGEANT I am the only witness, sir. I was drilling B Flight that morning.

FLIGHT LIEUTENANT Was the sound slight?

FLIGHT SERGEANT Rang across the parade ground, sir.

FLIGHT LIEUTENANT And was it—identifiable?

FLIGHT SERGEANT Very, sir.

FLIGHT LIEUTENANT I see. (*To* PARSONS) You don't dispute the actual word you used?

PARSONS No, sir.

FLIGHT LIEUTENANT Merely its volume?

PARSONS Whisper, sir.

FLIGHT LIEUTENANT But it was heard clearly by the Flight Sergeant.

PARSONS Might have lip-read, sir.

FLIGHT LIEUTENANT It's still swearing on parade, isn't it?

PARSONS Yes, sir.

FLIGHT LIEUTENANT And that's a serious offense. (*Looking down at the paper on his desk*) However, I'm glad to see it's your first. Still, that's not saying much after only ten weeks in the Service. (*To* FLIGHT SERGEANT) How is he at drill, generally?

FLIGHT SERGEANT He used to be in the Navy, sir.

FLIGHT LIEUTENANT Don't they order arms from the slope in the Navy?

PARSONS Yes, sir. But they do it proper time.

FLIGHT LIEUTENANT Careful, Parsons.

PARSONS Sorry, sir. I meant different time.

FLIGHT LIEUTENANT Well, you'll just have to get used to the timing we use here at the Depot—which is, anyway, exactly the same as the Guards. Also to learn to order arms properly without hitting your foot and swearing.

PARSONS Yes, sir.

FLIGHT LIEUTENANT Think yourself lucky I'm not putting this on your conduct sheet. All right. Accused admonished.

FLIGHT SERGEANT Prisoner and escort right turn, quick march, left right, left right. Halt. A.C.2 Parsons. Dismiss. (PARSONS *and his escort are marched out*)

FLIGHT LIEUTENANT Next.

FLIGHT SERGEANT (*Barking*) Prisoner and escort, attention, quick march, left right, left right, halt, left turn. Aircraftman Ross.
(*Another aircraftman has been marched in. The escorts are the same. The accused is a small man of thirty-five with a long face and a sad, shy expression. He speaks in a very gentle voice. His name is now Ross, and will, one day, be Shaw, but in the text he is designated by his first surname*)

FLIGHT LIEUTENANT (*Looking at the charge sheet*) 352087 A.C.2 Ross?

LAWRENCE Yes, sir.

FLIGHT LIEUTENANT (*Reading*) Conduct prejudicial to good order and Royal Air Force discipline in that the accused failed to report to the Guard Room by 2359 hours on December 16th, 1922, on expiry of his late pass issued on that date and did not in fact report until 0017 hours on December 17th, 1922. Period of unauthorized absence—eighteen minutes. (*He looks up at the* FLIGHT SERGEANT) Witness present?

FLIGHT SERGEANT Guard commander's report, sir.

FLIGHT LIEUTENANT (*Looking at another document*) Oh yes. Well, Ross. Anything to say?

LAWRENCE No, sir.

FLIGHT LIEUTENANT You admit the charge?

LAWRENCE Yes, sir.

FLIGHT LIEUTENANT (*Looking at another document*) I see you've been on two charges already. Untidy turn-out, three days' confined to camp, dumb insolence to an officer, seven days' confined to camp. So this charge makes the third in the ten weeks you've been in the Air Force. That's bad, Ross. That's very bad indeed. (*Suddenly thumping the desk*) Ross, I'm speaking to you. I said that's very bad indeed.

LAWRENCE I'm sorry, sir. I took it as an observation, not as a question. I agree, it's very bad indeed.

FLIGHT LIEUTENANT (*After a pause*) I've an idea you don't care for authority, Ross?

LAWRENCE I care for discipline, sir.

FLIGHT LIEUTENANT What's the distinction?

LAWRENCE Very wide, I believe.

FLIGHT LIEUTENANT Being late on pass is an offense against both authority and discipline, isn't it?

LAWRENCE Yes, sir. The point was academic.

FLIGHT LIEUTENANT (*After a pause*) What made you join the R.A.F.?

LAWRENCE I think I had a mental breakdown, sir.

FLIGHT LIEUTENANT (*More hurt than angry*) That kind of insolence isn't called for, Ross. I'm here not only to judge you but to help you. Will you try and understand that?

LAWRENCE Yes, sir.

FLIGHT LIEUTENANT All right. Let's start again. Why did you join the R.A.F.?

LAWRENCE (*Slowly*) Because I wanted to, because I was destitute, because I enjoy discipline, and because I had a mental breakdown. (*The* FLIGHT LIEUTENANT *stares at him, angrily*) If you prefer, sir, we can substitute for "mental"—the word "spiritual." I don't happen to like it myself, but at least it avoids the imputation of insolence.

FLIGHT LIEUTENANT (*To* FLIGHT SERGEANT) Flight?

FLIGHT SERGEANT Sir.

FLIGHT LIEUTENANT What is your report on this airman, in terms of general conduct?

FLIGHT SERGEANT Satisfactory, sir.

FLIGHT LIEUTENANT No signs of being bolshie—or general bloody-mindedness?

FLIGHT SERGEANT No, sir.

FLIGHT LIEUTENANT Drill?

FLIGHT SERGEANT Behind the others, sir, but then he's older and therefore slower. But he tries hard.

FLIGHT LIEUTENANT P/T?

FLIGHT SERGEANT According to the sergeant instructor, sir, he has difficulty in keeping up with the squad, but then his age comes into that too, and his—physical handicaps.

FLIGHT LIEUTENANT Physical handicaps? This is a recruit, Flight Sergeant, passed into the R.A.F. as A.1. What physical handicaps are you talking about?

FLIGHT SERGEANT (*Uneasily*) Well, sir. I only know that twice after P/T I've seen him being sick into a bucket, and he has some bad marks on his back, sir.

FLIGHT LIEUTENANT (*To* LAWRENCE) What are these marks?

LAWRENCE The scars of an accident, sir.

FLIGHT LIEUTENANT A serious accident?

LAWRENCE At the time it seemed so.

FLIGHT LIEUTENANT And you were passed as A.1?

LAWRENCE Yes, sir.

FLIGHT LIEUTENANT (*To* FLIGHT SERGEANT) It seems very mysterious to me. (*To* LAWRENCE) Where did you go last night?

LAWRENCE To a place in Buckinghamshire—near Taplow.

FLIGHT LIEUTENANT By bus or train?

LAWRENCE Motor bicycle.

FLIGHT LIEUTENANT I see. Why were you late?

LAWRENCE I fell off it.

FLIGHT LIEUTENANT Were you drunk?

LAWRENCE No, sir. I only drink water, and I'm rather particular about that.

FLIGHT LIEUTENANT How did you fall off?

LAWRENCE I was going through Denham rather fast, but with a good ten minutes in hand, when a dog ran out into the street and I swerved. A car coming the other way hit me, and I was left with very little bicycle. It became necessary to run, which, as the Flight Sergeant has just told you, I'm not as adept at as some.

FLIGHT LIEUTENANT (*After a pause*) When I asked you just now if you had anything to say in answer to this charge, you said no.

LAWRENCE Yes, sir.

FLIGHT LIEUTENANT You didn't think a motor-cycle accident might be taken as a possible excuse?

LAWRENCE No, sir. Only as a reason.

FLIGHT LIEUTENANT Another distinction?

LAWRENCE Yes, sir. Another wide one.
(*There is a pause*)

FLIGHT LIEUTENANT Ross, I hope you realize that most officers trying your case would, by now, have given you the maximum sentence, or remanded you to the Station Commander with an additional charge of insubordination.

LAWRENCE Yes, sir.

FLIGHT LIEUTENANT You think it's going to help your case if you impress me with the fact that you're an educated man. But that fact doesn't impress me at all—do you understand?

LAWRENCE Yes, sir.

FLIGHT LIEUTENANT There are plenty of educated men in the ranks of the R.A.F. nowadays. (*He looks suddenly from* LAWRENCE *to one of his escorts,* DICKINSON) You—escort—what's your name?

(DICKINSON *very smartly steps a pace forward and stamps his foot in parade-ground manner*)

DICKINSON Dickinson, sir.

FLIGHT LIEUTENANT I know something about you. You were at a public school, weren't you?

DICKINSON Yes, sir.

FLIGHT LIEUTENANT Weren't you also an officer in the Gunners?

DICKINSON Yes, sir. Captain. Wartime commission, of course.

FLIGHT LIEUTENANT At the front?

DICKINSON Yes, sir. Passchendaele and the big Hun push in March '18. I got a blighty there.

FLIGHT LIEUTENANT And why did you join the R.A.F.?

DICKINSON I got a job when I was demobbed, selling motor cars, but found I preferred Service life, sir. I consider the R.A.F. the Service of the future and, when they turned me down for a commission, I decided to join anyway and work my way up through the ranks.

(*His answer has plainly pleased the* FLIGHT LIEUTENANT, *who nods smilingly at him*)

FLIGHT LIEUTENANT I hope you will. All right, Dickinson. (DICKINSON *steps back to his place beside* LAWRENCE *with supreme smartness*) You see, Ross, this airman is in your flight, and there are many others with similar records in other recruit squads. Where were you at school?

LAWRENCE Oxford High School, sir.

FLIGHT LIEUTENANT Were you in the war?

LAWRENCE Yes, sir.

FLIGHT LIEUTENANT In what capacity?

LAWRENCE Oh—mostly—liaison work.

FLIGHT LIEUTENANT Liaison work? Where?

LAWRENCE (*After a slight hesitation*) The Middle East.

FLIGHT LIEUTENANT Where in the Middle East?

LAWRENCE Oh, all kinds of places.

FLIGHT LIEUTENANT You seem very vague about it.

LAWRENCE It was rather a vague kind of job.

FLIGHT LIEUTENANT (*Angrily*) For heaven's sake, man, you must have known what you were doing.

LAWRENCE Not very often, sir.

FLIGHT LIEUTENANT When you talk about mental break-down you don't happen to mean just plain mad, do you?

LAWRENCE Not certifiably so, sir.

FLIGHT LIEUTENANT You're in trouble of some kind?

LAWRENCE (*Quietly*) Yes, sir.

FLIGHT LIEUTENANT Bad trouble?

LAWRENCE It seems so, to me.

FLIGHT LIEUTENANT You mean when you tell other people they don't find it so bad?

LAWRENCE I don't tell other people, sir.

FLIGHT LIEUTENANT No one at all?

LAWRENCE No one at all.

FLIGHT LIEUTENANT If I sent the Flight Sergeant and the escort out now—would you tell it to me?

LAWRENCE No, sir.

FLIGHT LIEUTENANT (*After a pause*) Look here, Ross, I'm not just your Flight Commander. You've got to try and look on me as a sort of Dutch uncle. (*After another pause*) Well?

LAWRENCE The untellable—even to a sort of Dutch uncle —can't be told.
(There is a pause. The FLIGHT LIEUTENANT, *frustrated, looks down at his desk)*

FLIGHT LIEUTENANT Why did you go to this place in Buckinghamshire?

LAWRENCE To have a meal with some friends.

FLIGHT LIEUTENANT Close friends?

LAWRENCE Some of them.

FLIGHT LIEUTENANT Give me their names.

LAWRENCE *(Momentarily nonplused)* Their names, sir?

FLIGHT LIEUTENANT *(Barking)* Yes, their names.
(He has taken up a notebook and pencil)

LAWRENCE But have you the right—?

FLIGHT LIEUTENANT Yes, I have the right. *(Shouting)* I want these people's names *now*. That's an order, Ross.

LAWRENCE *(With a faint sigh)* Very well, sir. Lord and Lady Astor, Mr. and Mrs. George Bernard Shaw, the Archbishop of Canterbury—
(The FLIGHT LIEUTENANT *has thrown his pencil down)*

FLIGHT LIEUTENANT All right. You now have two charges

to answer—the present one and the one I'm putting you on tomorrow to be dealt with by the Group Captain—to wit —gross insubordination to your Flight Commander. On the present charge you get seven days' confined to camp. As for the second—well—I doubt if in future you're going to find much time to relax your troubled soul.

LAWRENCE No, sir. I don't think it needs that kind of relaxation—

FLIGHT LIEUTENANT (*Shouting*) That's enough, unless you want a court-martial. March him out, Flight.

FLIGHT SERGEANT Prisoner and escort right turn, quick march, left right, left right. Halt. Prisoner and escort, dismiss. (LAWRENCE, DICKINSON *and* NOLAN *march out. The* FLIGHT SERGEANT *turns at the door*) That is the last charge, sir.

FLIGHT LIEUTENANT (*Wearily*) Thank God for that. (*He collects the charge sheets from his desk and throws them into his "Out" tray. Then he looks up at the* FLIGHT SERGEANT) How's the Flight coming along generally?

FLIGHT SERGEANT About average, sir.

FLIGHT LIEUTENANT Think you'll make airmen of them?

FLIGHT SERGEANT Of a sort, sir.

FLIGHT LIEUTENANT (*With a sigh*) I know what you mean.

ROSS

Shocking lot we're getting these days. (*With a change of tone*) But keep your eye on that chap Dickinson. I like the look of him. He ought to do well.

FLIGHT SERGEANT Yes, sir.

FLIGHT LIEUTENANT (*Feelingly*) And give that cocky little bastard, Ross, hell.

FLIGHT SERGEANT Yes, sir.

(*He salutes magnificently, turns, stamping his feet as if to split his heelbones. The lights fade. In the darkness we hear the sound of a mouth organ playing and men's voices singing, softly and sentimentally, a popular song of the period "The Sheik of Araby"*)

SCENE TWO

Scene: Part of a yard in the depot. PARSONS, NOLAN *and* DICKINSON *are prominent among a small group of the other recruits, one of whom is playing a mouth organ while others, only intermittently visible, are singing or whistling gently to his accompaniment.* NOLAN *is talking to* PARSONS *while* DICKINSON *is sitting apart from the others, hands behind his head, eyes open, musing.*

NOLAN (*Excitedly*) But he did, Sailor. I promise you he did.

PARSONS (*Incredulously*) Archbishop of Canterbury? Rossie say a thing like that? Our Rossie? Oh no—

NOLAN But I was there, Sailor. I was escort. I heard him, clear as a bell. (*Indicating* DICKINSON) So did you, didn't you, Dickie-bird?

DICKINSON (*Without moving*) What?

NOLAN When our officer this morning said to Rossie, "Look here, my man, I want you to tell me who you went out with last night"—what a bloody nerve to ask such a thing, mind you—did Rossie say Mr. and Mrs. George Bernard Shaw and the Archbishop of Canterbury?

DICKINSON Yes. Also—Lord and Lady Astor.

NOLAN (*Triumphantly to* PARSONS) You see? You couldn't have done better yourself, Sailor. (*To* DICKINSON) Weren't you proud of him, Dickie-bird?

DICKINSON Not particularly.

PARSONS Ex-ruddy-officer himself. Can't bear lip to one of his own kind.

DICKINSON (*Quietly*) You know that's a bloody lie, Sailor.

PARSONS Why weren't you proud of him, then?

DICKINSON (*Without taking his eyes from the sky*) The Archbishop was enough. With the other names he overdid it.

(LAWRENCE *comes in, staggering under the weight of a garbage bin*)

PARSONS And what do you think you're doing, Rossie, old bean?

LAWRENCE There are still three left to fill in there.

PARSONS Yes, Rossie-boy, and left by my own instructions for a very good purpose, which is in case some bloody officer sticks his nose out here and says: "I see you bleeders have done your fatigue, so you can bleeding well do another."

LAWRENCE (*Contrite*) I'm sorry, Sailor. I should have thought.

PARSONS (*Kindly*) Yes, you should, shouldn't you? (*To* NOLAN) Ruddy marvel, isn't it? Reads Greek like it was the *Pink 'Un,* and don't know his bottom from Uxbridge Town Hall. (LAWRENCE *has turned to take the bin back again*) No, leave it there, for Gawd's sake. We don't want to have to fill it again. (*Helplessly*) Cripes!

LAWRENCE (*Flustered*) I'm sorry.

PARSONS Never mind. Never mind. (*He suddenly thrusts out his hand*) Rossie-boy—
(LAWRENCE *turns and looks at* PARSONS' *outstretched hand in bewilderment*)

NOLAN (*Explanatorily*) The Archbishop.

LAWRENCE (*Still bewildered*) The Archbishop?

PARSONS And Mr. and Mrs. George Bernard Shaw, and in spite of what Dickie-bird says—Lord and Lady ruddy Astor —and though you might have added the Dolly Sisters and Gaby Deslys, no one can think of everything at once and I congratulate you, Rossie-boy. B Flight is proud of you.

LAWRENCE (*Rather overwhelmed, and wincing at the force of* PARSONS' *famous handshake*) It wasn't much, really—

PARSONS (*To the others*) Salute our hero, boys. (*There is a mild and faintly ironic cheer, and a few bars, also ironic, of a triumphal march from the mouth-organist. Putting his arm around* LAWRENCE'S *shoulder)* Come and sing, Rossie. (*To the mouth-organist)* Give us the old Sheik again. (*The mouth organ starts up)*

LAWRENCE (*Timidly)* I'm afraid I don't know the words.

PARSONS (*Shocked)* Cor stuff me. You must be the only man in England who don't. (*To mouth-organist)* Know anything in Latin or Greek?

LAWRENCE I know Tipperary.

PARSONS (*To the others, with irony)* He knows Tipperary. (*To mouth-organist)* Tipperary.

(*The men begin to sing it,* PARSONS' *voice leading the others, but softly, because of fear of discovery.* LAWRENCE'S *voice, rather quavering, can be heard, proving that at least he does know the words. They finish a chorus and* PARSONS *starts "Pack Up Your Troubles."* LAWRENCE *suddenly and brusquely breaks away from* PARSONS' *friendly embrace and moves quickly away from the group, his back to them.* PARSONS *looks after him, rather surprised, but says nothing, continuing to sing. The* FLIGHT SERGEANT *comes in past* LAWRENCE *who turns quickly from him. The singing stops abruptly)*

FLIGHT SERGEANT What's the idea of the concert?

PARSONS We'd nearly finished fatigue, Flight.

FLIGHT SERGEANT Nearly isn't quite, is it? (*Pointing to*

bin) What's that doing here? And how many more is there to fill?

PARSONS Three, Flight.

FLIGHT SERGEANT Well, if you're smart and do 'em quickly I might find something else for you to do before supper. Jump to it now. Many hands make light work—

PARSONS Oh. I wish I'd said that. How *do* you think of 'em, Flight?

FLIGHT SERGEANT (*Automatically*) None of your lip, Parsons, now—unless you want a dose of jankers. (LAWRENCE *attempts to pick up the filled bin*) No. Not you, Ross. Nolan—Dickinson, you take that. Rest of you inside, at the double. Ross, stay here. (NOLAN *and* DICKINSON *take the bin from* LAWRENCE *and disappear, presumably towards the incinerator, in the opposite direction from the others, who also exit.* LAWRENCE *and the* FLIGHT SERGEANT *are left alone. The* FLIGHT SERGEANT *stares at* LAWRENCE *curiously for a moment*) They been picking on you again, son?

LAWRENCE No, Flight.

FLIGHT SERGEANT You don't ought to mind 'em so much.

LAWRENCE I don't mind them, Flight.

FLIGHT SERGEANT Listen, I've got eyes in my head, haven't I?

(LAWRENCE *lowers his, in embarrassment*)

LAWRENCE (*With a smile*) Flight, I'm sorry, but I'm afraid you've got it wrong. It was just that—suddenly—for the first time in five years I'd remembered what it was to feel life worth living.

(NOLAN *and* DICKINSON *come in,* NOLAN *with his hands in his pockets*)

FLIGHT SERGEANT (*Barking*) Hands out of your pockets, you.

NOLAN Sorry, Flight. Can we go now, Flight?

FLIGHT SERGEANT No. Get a broom and sweep up those leaves over there. (*He points off.* DICKINSON *turns to make himself inconspicuous*) And you, Dickinson. (*The men murmur* "Yes, Flight" *and go off the way they came. The* FLIGHT SERGEANT *looks at* LAWRENCE, *frowning. At length*) Yes. You've got it bad, all right, haven't you? Real bad. (*Smiling*) Don't worry, I'm not young "greaser." I'm not going to ask you what your trouble is.

LAWRENCE Young "greaser"?

FLIGHT SERGEANT Flight Lieutenant Stoker to you. (*In "officer" accent*) "I'm not just here to judge you, you know, my man. I'm here to help you. Look on me as a sort of Dutch uncle, old fruit." Makes you bloody vomit.

LAWRENCE It does, rather.

FLIGHT SERGEANT Mind you, I didn't say that and nor did you.

LAWRENCE No, Flight.

FLIGHT SERGEANT One day, if you want to tell me what's up with you, you can and I'll listen. If you don't, that's all right too. Meanwhile I've got to try and stop young greaser from having you hung, drawn and quartered— (*The men have begun to come out of the building carrying the bins*) All right. At the double. And afterwards you can dismiss. But don't let anyone see you or I'll personally screw all your—

PARSONS Isn't our Flight Sergeant the best little Flight Sergeant in the world? Say yes, boys, or it'll seem rude.

FLIGHT SERGEANT (*Shouting*) That's quite enough of that. (*To* LAWRENCE) All right. I'll do what I can. (*Suddenly roaring*) But don't ever let me hear you being insubordinate to your Flight Commander like that again, do you hear?

LAWRENCE Yes, Flight.

FLIGHT SERGEANT (*To the corner, whither* DICKINSON *and* NOLAN *have disappeared*) All right, you two. *Fini.* But keep out of sight of any bleeding officer, if you please. (*He goes out. After a moment* DICKINSON *and* NOLAN *come on.* DICKINSON *puts a broom against a wall and having done that turns and languidly looks at* LAWRENCE, *who has taken out a small notebook in which he is writing, squatting on the ground, with his legs tucked under his body.* NOLAN *approaches* LAWRENCE)

NOLAN Rossie?

LAWRENCE Yes, Paddy?

NOLAN (*With acute embarrassment*) I wouldn't be asking this at all, but I thought perhaps—well—you're not the same as the rest of us and perhaps pay parade doesn't mean to you as much as it means to some of us, and—

LAWRENCE I'm afraid it does, Paddy. Quite as much.

NOLAN (*Overwhelmed with remorse*) Oh, but, then, please you must not on any account—

LAWRENCE How much would it have been?

NOLAN Well, it was a ring you see—something I had to buy —you know—to make it up with my girl, you see, and she likes the best, always has—thirty-seven and six.

LAWRENCE I wish I had it, Paddy.
(NOLAN *looks over at* DICKINSON, *who, almost imperceptibly, shakes his head*)

NOLAN (*With a sigh*) Oh well.
(*He goes sadly out.* LAWRENCE *continues to write in his notebook. Pause.* DICKINSON *walks slowly forward*)

DICKINSON Why do you sit like that?

LAWRENCE I always do.

DICKINSON It's the way the Arabs sit, isn't it?

LAWRENCE I don't know.

DICKINSON (*Squatting beside him*) But you should know—shouldn't you—after all that liaison work you did in the Middle East in the last war?

LAWRENCE I'm sorry. I wasn't paying attention. Yes, it's the way the Arabs sit.

DICKINSON Damned uncomfortable it looks. Why are you shivering?

LAWRENCE I've got a touch of malaria.

DICKINSON Middle East, I suppose? You're shaking quite badly. You'd better see the M.O.

LAWRENCE No. I'll have a temperature tonight and tomorrow it'll be gone.

DICKINSON Yes, but you shouldn't take risks, old chap. After all, we don't want to lose you, do we?

LAWRENCE I doubt if B Flight would notice.

DICKINSON I wasn't talking about B Flight. I was talking about the nation. (LAWRENCE *puts down the notebook at last, and stares steadily at* DICKINSON) Aren't you going to say "What on earth do you mean?" Aren't you going to try and act it out just a little longer? (*Pause.* LAWRENCE, *staring at him steadily, says nothing*) I agree old boy. Useless. At the same time I notice you're not falling into the trap of saying "How on earth did you find out?" and so confirming what might, after all, be only a wild guess. Secret Agent training, no doubt. Well, it isn't a guess. It *was* until this morning, I grant. As a matter of fact I did see you once, in Paris, in 1919—Peace Conference time—I was just a humble captain, walking down a street and suddenly I was shoved back against some railings by some brawny gendarmes and practically squashed to death by an hysterical crowd because *you* were leaving your hotel. I couldn't see you well, but *I* remember you walking shyly—oh so shyly—between two policemen—to your car, head well down under that Arab headdress and then—at the car—turning to talk to someone so that the crowd grew even more hysterical, and then, when you were in the car, modestly pulling down the blind. Still, I wouldn't necessarily have recognized you, old boy, from that—nor even from the lecture I went to at the Albert Hall, which was supposed to be about the Palestine Campaign, but which had your picture on every other slide—very carefully posed, old boy, I hope you don't mind my saying. (*He offers a cigarette to* LAWRENCE, *who shakes his head silently.* DICKINSON *lights one for himself*) Still think I'm guessing? Look, old chap, it isn't awfully hard—even for a humble airman like me—to find out the telephone number of Cliveden House, to ring up and ask if there'd been a raincoat left behind last night by Colonel Lawrence. "Colonel Lawrence, sir?" Well-trained, this footman evidently. "Yes, for heaven's sake—Colonel Lawrence—my dear man— Oh, very well, then, Aircraftman Ross, if you like." Slight pause. Then "No, sir. The Colonel left nothing behind last night. In fact I distinctly remember when he left that he had his raincoat strapped onto the back of his motor bicycle." (*Pause*) Your hand really *is* shaking badly. I honestly think you'd better see the M.O., old boy. After all, you can't do punishment drill with malaria.

LAWRENCE (*In a low voice*) What do you want from me?

DICKINSON (*Genially*) Money.

LAWRENCE I haven't any.

DICKINSON (*Murmuring*) Oh yes. Destitute. I enjoyed that this morning.

LAWRENCE It was the truth.

DICKINSON (*Hurt*) Don't treat me like a half-wit, old boy. I'm not like the others. *I* can use the old gray matter, you know. I can tell how much money a man with your name could make for himself if he tried. Your memoirs? God! They'd make you a bloody fortune, and don't tell me you're not writing them, old boy, because I've seen you scribbling away in that notebook when you think no one's looking.

LAWRENCE What I'm writing is for my friends. It's not for money.

DICKINSON Jolly noble. Well a bit of it had better be for money, old boy, because to keep my trap shut about this little masquerade of yours, you're going to have to pay me

a hundred quid. That's what I reckon I could get from Fleet Street— (LAWRENCE *shakes his head*) Listen, I haven't an earthly what you're up to, old boy, and I don't care either. Hiding? Spying? Having fun? Doesn't concern me. But it must be damned important to you that I don't give the story to the papers. So let's not haggle. Seventy-five, and I'll take a check.
(*There is a pause*)

LAWRENCE (*At length*) No.

DICKINSON You mean that?

LAWRENCE Yes.

DICKINSON (*With a sigh*) Oh well, I thought you mightn't fork out. You were so damn careless this morning with young greaser, that I felt pretty sure you must have finished whatever it was you came into this thing to do—

LAWRENCE (*Suddenly fierce*) I haven't finished. I haven't even started.

DICKINSON What *did* you come into this thing to do?

LAWRENCE To find peace.
(*A pause; then* DICKINSON *laughs quietly*)

DICKINSON Oh yes—the mental and spiritual breakdown—

LAWRENCE Go and telephone the papers—

DICKINSON Oh, I'm not ringing them up. This transaction's got to be strictly cash.

LAWRENCE You'll go and see them?

DICKINSON Yes.

LAWRENCE When?

DICKINSON Tonight.

LAWRENCE Have you got a late pass?

DICKINSON No. Just ways of egress and ingress.

LAWRENCE (*Bitterly*) I see. Well, have fun tomorrow with the headlines.

DICKINSON Don't tell me you're frightened of headlines, old boy.

LAWRENCE I am now. Oh yes, you spotted my enjoyment of that crowd in Paris and this morning too—showing off to the Flight Lieutenant, but forgetting all about the sharp-witted escort who was going to end my life—

DICKINSON Suicide threat?

LAWRENCE No. Statement of fact. I mean my life as Aircraftman Ross.

DICKINSON What does that matter? Lawrence will still be alive.

LAWRENCE (*With anger*) Lawrence doesn't exist any more. If you kill Aircraftman Ross you kill me. Can I put it more simply than that?
(*There is a pause*)

DICKINSON I don't scare very easily, you know.

LAWRENCE I'm sure you don't. I wish I didn't.

DICKINSON (*Angrily*) Why the hell is all this so important to you?

LAWRENCE Why is a monastery important to the man who takes refuge in it?

DICKINSON A monastery is for someone who's lost his will to live. (*Angrily*) All right. The spiritual breakdown. I'll buy it. How did you lose your soul?

LAWRENCE The way most people lose it, I suppose. By worshiping a false god.

DICKINSON What god?

LAWRENCE The will.

DICKINSON The thing that's up in your head, you mean?

LAWRENCE The thing that *was* up in my head.

DICKINSON Isn't that what's made you what you are?

LAWRENCE Yes.

DICKINSON I meant Lawrence of Arabia.

LAWRENCE I meant Ross of Uxbridge.

DICKINSON (*Hotly*) Self-pity—that's all it is. There's nothing in the world worse than self-pity—

LAWRENCE Oh, yes there is. Self-knowledge. Why shouldn't a man pity himself if to him he is pitiable? But to know yourself—or rather to be shown yourself—as you really are— (*He breaks off*) Yes. How stupid those ancient Greeks were. With your public school education I'm sure you'd understand what I mean. Can I borrow a couple of pounds? (DICKINSON *takes out his wallet and extracts two pound notes from it. Then he walks over to* LAWRENCE *and hands them to him*) Thank you. That proves it. You're going to do it.

DICKINSON Good psychology. Yes, I'm going to do it, all right—because I'm damn well not going to be cheated out of money I need by a bit of fake playacting—

LAWRENCE Aren't you confusing Ross with Lawrence? Or is Ross a fake too? Perhaps you're right. It doesn't matter much anyway. Fake or not he's been a dreadful failure. Lets the Flight down at drill and P/T, can't tell a dirty joke to save his life and never sees the point of one either, talks la-de-da and spoils any party by trying too hard. Still, just now, with Sailor and Tipperary I thought it was just possible— (*He breaks off*) No. That was sloppy thinking.

Ross dies tomorrow and he'll be better dead. (*He looks dispassionately at his shaking hand, then up at* DICKINSON, *with a quick smile*) Do you really think the papers will pay you a hundred?

DICKINSON More, perhaps.

LAWRENCE Really? You will tell me how much they *do* pay, won't you?

(*He turns and goes out. The lights fade. In the darkness we hear the distant sound of the "Last Post"*)

SCENE THREE

Scene: A hut. Four beds are visible. PARSONS *lies on one in his underclothes. He is working out racing results from an evening paper.* NOLAN *lies on another, in pajamas. He is writing a letter.*

PARSONS Paddy—what's five to four, doubled with seven to two?

NOLAN Sorry, Sailor, I'm not a racing man. (*Bent over his letter*) You tell me something.

PARSONS (*Bent over his calculations*) What?

NOLAN Another word for love. (PARSONS *looks at him morosely without replying. Explosively*) Love, love, love. Man, you get sick of it. I tell you. (*Waving letter*) Don't you know another word?

PARSONS Who's it to?

NOLAN My girl. The one I'm marrying.

PARSONS That Schoolmaster's daughter? (NOLAN *nods*) I don't know another word.

NOLAN But she's different, you know, Sailor. Not at all what you'd imagine. Free-thinking, that's what she is—

PARSONS (*Muttering*) Free-doing, too, I hope.

NOLAN You'd be surprised.

(DICKINSON *comes in and goes to one of the unoccupied beds*)

PARSONS Ah. Dickie-bird—you'd know. What's five to four, doubled with seven to two in shillings?

DICKINSON Let's see. Eight and fourpence halfpenny.

PARSONS (*Admiringly*) Now that's the sort of brainwork I appreciate—not— (*He nods his head disparagingly towards the fourth bed*) I'll bet *you* don't read Greek poetry in the lats, Dickie-bird.

DICKINSON You're damn right, I don't, old boy. The *Police Gazette's* about my level.

(LAWRENCE *comes in and goes to the fourth bed, passing* DICKINSON *as he does so.* DICKINSON *is lying on his bed, fully dressed and does not look at* LAWRENCE, *who begins to take his jacket off with evidently rather uncertain fingers.* LAWRENCE *suddenly seems to remember something. He walks across to* NOLAN, *takes two pounds out of his trouser pocket and hands them to him*)

LAWRENCE Have you got half-a-crown?

NOLAN But you said you didn't have it.

LAWRENCE (*Not looking at* DICKINSON) I managed to raise it.

NOLAN Oh Ross, you shouldn't have. Will he wait—your man?

LAWRENCE I'm sure he will.

NOLAN For how long?

LAWRENCE I should think—for eternity.

NOLAN (*Handing him half-a-crown*) Pay day after next you shall have it back. It's a promise. And one day—

LAWRENCE That's all right.

NOLAN (*Back to his letter*) Rossie—you'd know. Aren't there any other words for love, except love, in the English? Think of something to surprise her—

LAWRENCE I'm not an expert.

NOLAN Try.

LAWRENCE Tenderness, devotion, the communion of two spirits—

NOLAN (*Doubtfully*) A bit tame.

LAWRENCE I'm sorry—

PARSONS (*Who has been staring at* LAWRENCE, *frowning*) Hey. What's the matter with you?

LAWRENCE Nothing.

(*He goes to his bed.* PARSONS *follows him*)

PARSONS You're shaking like a ruddy shimmy dancer. The sweats, too. Got a dose of something?

(LAWRENCE *does not answer.* DICKINSON *answers for him, quietly*)

DICKINSON Malaria.

PARSONS Malaria?

LAWRENCE It's all right, Sailor. It's not catching.

PARSONS I don't care if it is or it isn't. I'm the senior here and I'm not taking no chances. (*Peremptorily, as* LAWRENCE *continues silently to undress*) Put your things on again and go and report sick. Don't play "silly bleeders" now—

(*He thrusts* LAWRENCE's *tunic towards him roughly, trying to maneuver his arm into the sleeve*)

LAWRENCE (*Quietly, but in a voice of sudden, unmistakable authority*) Take your hands off me.

PARSONS (*Bewildered*) What you say?

LAWRENCE I dislike being touched.

(*He takes his jacket from* PARSONS, *and hangs it up*)

PARSONS Listen, Ross. I'm telling you to report sick.

LAWRENCE (*Still quietly, but with the same authority*) I'm not going to report sick. I'm going to sleep it off here. (*He lies down on the bed, half-undressed, shivering, and pulls the blanket over him*)

PARSONS I'm warning you, my lad, if you're not reporting sick tonight, you're doing your bleeding P/T tomorrow morning–malaria or no malaria. *Compris?*

LAWRENCE (*Half-asleep*) *Compris.*

PARSONS Enjoy torturing yourself by any chance?

LAWRENCE It's a fair comment, I suppose. Goodnight, Sailor. If I make too much noise in the night, wake me up.

PARSONS I'll keep a boot handy. (*Defeated, he turns to* DICKINSON *who is still lying, fully dressed, on his bed*) And what do you think you're doing? Going to sleep like that? (DICKINSON *gives him a lazy wink*) What again? (DICKINSON *nods*) Who is she tonight?

DICKINSON No she tonight. Business.

PARSONS Funny time for business.

DICKINSON It's funny business.

PARSONS Well, for God's sake don't get caught.

DICKINSON I won't.

PARSONS *(Lowering his voice)* I'll expect the usual half-nicker.

DICKINSON You might get a whole nicker if things go right.

PARSONS I'll believe that when I see it.
(The lights go out suddenly)

NOLAN *(With a wail)* Oh no. Just when I'd got sort of inspired. I won't remember it tomorrow.

PARSONS What?

NOLAN A time we were together one night on a beach near Galway.

PARSONS You'll remember it tomorrow.

NOLAN Not the words I was using—

PARSONS You'll be remembering some other words if you don't put a sock in it.

NOLAN But the words were good, Sailor—

PARSONS Pipe down, you sex-mad Celt. 'Night, all.

NOLAN }
DICKINSON } 'Night, Sailor.

(After a moment of silence and near darkness, DICKINSON *quietly gets up from his bed and moves on tiptoe towards the door. He stops a second by* LAWRENCE'S *bed*

and looks down. Then he goes on. LAWRENCE *suddenly flings out his arm in a pleading gesture)*

LAWRENCE (*Murmuring*) No. No—
(DICKINSON *stops and turns back)*

DICKINSON (*In a whisper*) Speaking to me, old boy? (*There is no answer, save a faint moan. It is plain that* LAWRENCE *was talking in his sleep*) Happy dreams—Colonel—
(*He tiptoes cautiously to the door, opens it a fraction, peeps out furtively, and then quickly slips from sight, closing the door behind him. The lights die to a complete black-out in the hut.*

After a pause we hear a muffled roll of drums and the opening bars of "Land of Hope and Glory" played by an organ, but coming apparently from a distance. As the lights gradually come on we find that a large magic-lantern screen has been lowered, on which is a photograph of LAWRENCE *in spotlessly white Arab dress, with a large, curved, ornamental dagger around his waist. He is lying on the ground, a rifle by his side, gazing thoughtfully into space. A camel squats sleepily behind him. The desert background looks decidedly unreal and the whole effect is phony and posed. In front of the screen is a lecturer,* FRANKS, *in dinner jacket)*

FRANKS This is the man. The Colonel himself—perhaps the most legendary figure of modern times—the scholar-soldier—the uncrowned King of the Desert—wearing, as you see (*He points to* LAWRENCE'*s dagger*) the insignia of a Prince of Mecca—an honor awarded him by Prince

Abdullah— (*He breaks off and speaks testily to the unseen R.A.F. hut*) Surely this is what you always wanted?

LAWRENCE'S VOICE (*Actual, not recorded*) Not now. Now I only want you to tell them the truth.

FRANKS But what is the truth? Does anyone know? Ah—Field-Marshal. (*A man whom we are later to meet as* ALLENBY *appears from the darkness beside* FRANKS) What was your view of Lawrence?

ALLENBY Well, I was never too sure how much of a charlatan he was. Quite a bit, I should think. Still, there's no disputing the greatness of what he did.
(FRANKS *turns to the other side of the stage where another figure, a civilian in tropical clothes, has become visible*)

FRANKS And you, Mr. Storrs?

STORRS I think the importance of what he did has perhaps been exaggerated—by the press, by people like you and—to be fair—by himself. It's in what he *was* that he was great—in my view, probably the greatest Englishman of his time.
(*A British Brigadier-General,* BARRINGTON, *in tropical uniform appears on the opposite side of the stage*)

FRANKS Ah. General. You knew Lawrence, didn't you?

BARRINGTON Oh, very well. Couldn't bear him. Awful little show-off—quite a bit of a sadist, too. Cold-blooded. No feelings. Doubt if his private life would bear much

looking into, either. As for what he did—well, a lot of chaps did just as well, but didn't get the publicity.
(The splendidly dressed figure of AUDA ABU TAYI *stalks onto the stage, shouldering* BARRINGTON *contemptuously out of the way)*

AUDA *(Thunderously)* Tell them in England what I—Auda Abu Tayi—say of el Aurans. Of Manhood—the man. Of Freedom—free. A spirit without equal. I see no flaw in him.

LAWRENCE *(From the darkness, agonizedly)* No flaw?

AUDA I see no flaw in him.
(He stalks away into the darkness. A man in the uniform of a Turkish General approaches the screen, but remains silent, looking towards the hut)

FRANKS You see how difficult it is. Where *is* the truth? They can't all be right, can they? I really think it's safe to stick to the simple story—that boy scout epic of yours. You're a legend, you see—and I mustn't spoil it for the public. They want Lawrence—not Ross. They want a world hero, not a fever-stricken recruit, sick of life, sick of himself, on the threshold of self-ending. *(To the* TURKISH GENERAL*)* Who are you? Are you part of the great Lawrence story?

GENERAL Not of the legend. But I'm part of the truth. *(Behind* LAWRENCE's *bed, looking down)* But don't worry, my friend. I won't tell. I never have and I never will.

LAWRENCE (*Off*) One day I will.

GENERAL (*Politely*) Will you indeed? I never denied your bravery. But that would really be *very* brave—
(*The* GENERAL *goes into the darkness*)

FRANKS (*Relieved*) That's enough of that unsavory nonsense. Next slide, please. (*A large map of the Middle East [pre-1914 war] is flashed onto the screen*) In 1916 the whole of this vast area (*He points*) was under the domination of the Turkish Empire, with which the Allies were at war. (*He points again*) The Turks were menacing the Suez Canal, and the British were too weak to attempt a counteroffensive. The great battle of the Somme had just cost them nearly half a million casualties, with no result. The whole vast war had bogged down in a morass of blood—and there seemed no way for either side to win. However, on June the fifth, 1916, an event occurred down here (*He points to Mecca*) on which the newspapers barely deigned to comment, although it was later to change the world's history. The Sherif of Mecca revolted against the Turks, captured their garrisons at Mecca and Jeddah, and with his sons the Princes Feisal and Abdullah challenged the might of the vast Turkish Empire with his tiny force of Bedouin tribesmen. Disaster, of course, would have followed, but on October the sixteenth, 1916, there landed at Jeddah (*He points*) two Englishmen—one a mature, clever and far-seeing diplomat —Ronald Storrs—and the other—next slide, please— (*A photograph of* LAWRENCE *is flashed onto the screen. He is in Army uniform [Captain] looking sternly and soulfully straight into the camera lens*) A young man—filled with an implacable devotion to the cause of Arab unity, and a stern sense of duty to his own country—(*From the darkness there is a gentle laugh*) What's the matter?

LAWRENCE (*Off*) You make it all sound so dull.

FRANKS Dull?

LAWRENCE (*Off*) Yes. It wasn't like that at all. Not in the beginning. It was fun.

FRANKS (*Sternly*) Fun, Aircraftman Ross?

LAWRENCE (*Off*) Yes. In the beginning—

(*The lights fade. There is the sound of Arab martial music, jaunty and barbaric, but not at all stern and military. Interposed are the sounds of shouting and laughter*)

Scene four

Scene: The interior of an Arab tent. As the lights come on, LAWRENCE *is being helped into an imposing-looking white Arab gown by a ferocious-looking, plainly disapproving Arab servant* (HAMED). *Another servant* (RASHID), *younger and gentler-seeming than the first, holds a mirror for* LAWRENCE *to look into.* STORRS *sits on a stool, smoking a cigar. The Arab music continues.*

LAWRENCE (*Surveying himself*) Storrs, how do I look?

STORRS The most Anglo-Saxon Arab I ever saw.

LAWRENCE That's all right. In Syria, before the war—when on archeological jaunts—I used to pass as a Circassian.

STORRS May I remind you we're about a thousand miles south of Damascus. Have you ever heard of a Circassian in the Hejaz?

LAWRENCE (*Still distracted by his appearance*) No. I can't say I have. Still, *one* might have wandered— (*The noise of martial music subsides*) The parade must be over. I told Abdullah his men were shooting off far too many bullets that should be kept for the Turks. If I can't say Circassian, what *shall* I say?

STORRS If I were you I'd say you were an English Intelligence Captain on leave from Cairo, going on an unauthorized visit to Prince Feisal's headquarters, through country that no Christian has ever crossed before. They can't possibly believe you and so all they may do is to make a small incision in your skull to let the devil of madness out. It hurts quite a lot, I believe—but at least there's a chance of survival—

LAWRENCE Don't you think I need something round the waist?

STORRS What sort of something?

LAWRENCE I don't know. Some sort of ornament. A dagger for instance. I'm supposed to be dressed as a great lord of the desert, you see. Abdullah thinks that the more conspicuous I look, the less attention I'll cause, which is rather sensible—don't you think? (*To* HAMED) Go to the Lord Abdullah and beg him in the name of Allah to lend to his servant Captain Lawrence a dagger that would befit a Prince of Mecca. (HAMED *stares angrily at him for a moment, then turns and goes*) He seems to do what I tell him, which is a comfort. I hope the others do—

STORRS What others?

LAWRENCE Abdullah also wants me to take some of his own men to reinforce his brother—

STORRS Now I put your chance of survival at zero. The

minute they're out of sight of Abdullah's camp they'll slit your infidel throat.

LAWRENCE That's what Abdullah thinks too. (*He begins to walk up and down*) A sheik walks differently from ordinary mortals.

STORRS (*Unhappily*) I ought to stop you from going.

LAWRENCE You can't, and well you know it. I don't come under you.

STORRS Seriously, T.E., the risks are out of all proportion to any good you think you can do. Oh yes—I know it'll be fun for you if you get back to Cairo to infuriate the senior officers by telling them that they've got their facts all wrong—that you've inspected the situation at first hand and *know*. But I honestly don't think you will get back to Cairo—

LAWRENCE When I was an undergraduate I wanted to write a thesis on crusader castles. So I went to Syria alone, without money, in the height of summer, and walked twelve hundred miles in three months. I was completely dependent on the Arab laws of hospitality. People said then they didn't think I'd get back to Oxford—

STORRS (*Impatiently*) This isn't Syria. This is their Holy Land. Down here the Arab laws of hospitality don't extend to Christians. It's their religious duty to kill you—

LAWRENCE Ah—but I have a bodyguard—don't forget.

STORRS A bodyguard? You mean that thug over there—and his murderous-looking friend—

LAWRENCE Oh, I don't think Rashid is a thug. I even got him to speak to me. He spat afterwards, of course, to clean his mouth, but in quite a polite way. I admit I haven't yet had the same success with Hamed, but I won't give up trying.
(STORRS *gets up suddenly and goes up to* LAWRENCE)

STORRS (*Touching his arm*) T.E. (LAWRENCE *withdraws his arm quickly*) You might easily get killed.

LAWRENCE I might easily get run over by a staff motor in Cairo.

STORRS Why are you really doing this? (*As* LAWRENCE *opens his mouth*) Don't tell me any more about that mysterious kinship you feel with the Arab race. I don't believe it. You don't love the Arabs. You happen to speak their language and get on with them, but you're not a mystic like Burton or Doughty. You're doing this for some very personal reason. What is it?

LAWRENCE (*After a pause and speaking with far more weight than his words*) I need air. (*Before* STORRS *can reply* HAMED *comes in with an ornamental belt and dagger which he brusquely hands to* LAWRENCE. *With a winning smile*) May Allah bless you, Hamed, friend of my heart and guardian of my life— (HAMED *turns his back and walks away with great dignity to stand beside* RASHID. *Shrugging*) Oh well. Everything takes time. (*Showing* STORRS *the dagger*) I say, Storrs—look at this. Isn't this splendid? (*He begins to put it on, with apparent glee*) Rashid, hold the mirror up again. (RASHID *does so*) By jove, yes. With this I shall really be one of the lords of the desert— (BARRINGTON *comes into the tent, dressed in tropical uniform. He looks hot and bad-tempered*)

BARRINGTON Storrs?

(STORRS *has got up with alacrity.* LAWRENCE *has glanced quickly over his shoulder at the new arrival, and then reverts to his image in the mirror*)

STORRS Ah, Colonel. It's good to see you again.

BARRINGTON I'm sorry I wasn't on the quay to meet you. The message from H.Q. about your arrival came late. How did you find your way to Abdullah's camp?

STORRS Captain Lawrence found some man to guide us—

BARRINGTON But that's very dangerous, you know, out here —strictly against regulations, too. And who's Captain Lawrence?

STORRS (*Helplessly*) He's over there.

LAWRENCE (*Turning, affably*) How do you do. You're Colonel Barrington, aren't you, our representative in Jeddah.

BARRINGTON Yes. I am.

LAWRENCE Tell me, what do you think of Abdullah?

BARRINGTON (*Bewildered*) What do I think of His Highness? Well, I think he's an exceptionally able and gifted person—

LAWRENCE Exactly. He's too able and gifted to see anything except defeat. I don't blame him for that, but I don't think he's really our man—do you? I'm putting my money on Feisal.

BARRINGTON Are you?

LAWRENCE Ah. You probably see Feisal as a fool because he thinks he can win, and, of course, if he merely *thinks* that, then, I agree, he is a fool. But if—just by some strange chance—he happened to believe it, then—well, he'd be our man, wouldn't he? It seems to me worth a trip, anyway. Excuse me, but I really must make use of as much daylight as possible. Hamed, Rashid, tell the men to make ready and mount. (HAMED *and* RASHID *disappear silently.* LAWRENCE *turns to* STORRS) Well, goodbye, Storrs. I'll see you in about a month.

BARRINGTON Are you intending to ride to Feisal? Is that the meaning of this rig-out?

LAWRENCE It is a bit peculiar, isn't it? At first Abdullah wanted to disguise me as a woman, with a yashmak, but I thought that was going a bit too far. Also—sort of cheating too, don't you think?

BARRINGTON Do you happen to realize the risks involved?

LAWRENCE Oh yes. We've been into all that.

BARRINGTON But do you know anything about the sort of country between here and the Wadi Safru?

LAWRENCE A bit rough, I'm told.

BARRINGTON Are you? Well, this is what *I'm* told. Bare desert without any shelter at all, for three days. Then four days climbing a virtually impassable range of mountains, another two days climbing down it, and then another three days across an even worse desert. Then— (*He breaks off.* LAWRENCE *is counting up on his fingers*) What are you doing?

LAWRENCE You've already made it twelve days. Quite frankly, Colonel, I'll be disappointed if we don't do it in six—
(*He goes out*)

BARRINGTON Who on earth *is* that awful little pip-squeak?

STORRS Lawrence? My super-cerebral little companion? He's from the Arab Bureau in Cairo—

BARRINGTON Ah, he's one of *that* menagerie, is he? Why was he sent out here?

STORRS He wasn't. He just came.

BARRINGTON Good Lord. Unauthorized? (STORRS *nods*) What's his job in the Arab Bureau?

STORRS Making maps.

BARRINGTON Fine lot of use that's going to be to him.

STORRS I don't know. His maps are very good.

BARRINGTON Very artistic, I've no doubt—with the desert a tasteful yellow, and the mountains a pretty shade of mauve. (*Angrily*) Listen, Storrs—I don't want to have anything to do with this business. I know nothing about it whatever—do you understand?

STORRS Yes. Very clearly.

BARRINGTON From now on Captain precious Lawrence of the Arab Bureau is entirely on his own—

STORRS Yes, I think he'd prefer it that way.
(*The lights fade. We hear the sound of a man singing an Arab song, quietly, from a distance*)

SCENE FIVE

Scene: A desert place. There is no feature except a rock against which LAWRENCE *reclines, writing in a notebook. The rest is sky and a burning sun. Beside* LAWRENCE *lies* RASHID, *flat on his back.* HAMED *is asleep, some distance away.*

LAWRENCE What music is that, Rashid?

RASHID It is the music of an Howeitat song, el Aurans, in praise of Auda Abu Tayi.
(*He spits surreptitiously*)

LAWRENCE A noble man. They do well to honor him.

RASHID (*Surprised*) Even in Cairo they know of Auda?
(*He spits again*)

LAWRENCE Even in Cairo *I* know of Auda. Seventy-five blood enemies killed by his own hand, and all his tribesmen wounded in his service at least once. Assuredly the greatest warrior in all Arabia. (*Wistfully*) What an ally he would make to Feisal!

RASHID The Turks pay him too much money. He is a great man but he loves money. How is it you know so much about our country and our people, el Aurans?
(*He spits again*)

LAWRENCE (*Mildly*) Rashid, for the last five days I have wondered much whether Allah might not forgive you if, in conversation with me, you saved everything up for just one great spit at the end?

RASHID Don't tell Hamed or he will beat me. He is angry that I speak to you at all.

LAWRENCE Your guilty secret will be safe, I swear.

RASHID Answer my question, then, el Aurans.

LAWRENCE How do I know so much about your country and your people? Because I have made it my business to learn.

RASHID Why do you, an Englishman and a Christian, seek to serve our cause?

LAWRENCE Because in serving your country I also serve my own. Because in serving your cause I serve the cause of freedom. And in serving you I serve myself.

RASHID The last I don't understand.

LAWRENCE I don't quite understand it myself. (*He gets to his feet*) The hour is nearly finished. In ten minutes you must rouse the others.

RASHID (*Groaning*) Oh no, el Aurans. The sun is still too high—

LAWRENCE We must reach Prince Feisal's camp tonight.

RASHID You will kill us all. For five days we have had no rest. Look at Hamed there. (*He points to the sleeping bodyguard*) Never have I known him so weary. And I, I am a dying man, el Aurans.

LAWRENCE Resurrect yourself, then, corpse. (*He playfully prods him with his rifle;* RASHID, *smiling, staggers to his feet, overplaying his weariness*) Are you, Bedouins of the desert, to be put to shame by a man who, until a week ago, had spent two years of his life astride an office stool in Cairo. I am ashamed to lead so weak and effeminate a band—

RASHID (*With a giggle*) Who was it who yesterday had to hold you on your camel—to save you from falling down that ravine through weariness?

LAWRENCE It was you, Rashid, and I thank you. But I would not have fallen.

RASHID Allah would not have saved you.

LAWRENCE No.

RASHID Who then?

LAWRENCE The only god I worship. (*He taps his head*) It lives up here in this malformed temple and it is called —the will. (*Looking at* HAMED) Surely Hamed will kill me for bringing him from such a happy dream.

RASHID Let him dream on, el Aurans. And let me join him. *(He sinks to the ground in pretended exhaustion)*

LAWRENCE *(Gently)* You are with him in everything else, Rashid. I think at least you should allow him the solitude of his own dream. And it can only last another seven minutes.

RASHID *(Pleadingly)* El Aurans, why not wait until the evening? What do five hours matter?

LAWRENCE They can make the difference between winning and losing a war.

RASHID A war? *(Pityingly)* Forgive me, el Aurans, but I am an Arab and you are an Englishman and you do not understand. For five days I have heard you talk of an Arab war, but there *is* no war. We fight the Turks because we hate them, and we kill them when we can and where we can, and then when we have killed we go home. You speak of the Arab nation—but there *is* no Arab nation. My tribe is the Harif, and our neighbors are the Masruh. We are blood enemies. If I kill a Turk when I might have killed a man of the Masruh, I commit a crime against my tribe and my blood. And are the Harif and the Masruh the only blood enemies in Arabia? How then can we be a nation, and have an army? And without an army, how can we fight a war against the Turks? When you speak of the Arab war you dream foolish dreams, el Aurans—

LAWRENCE Very well. I dream foolish dreams. *(Looking at his watch)* Five minutes and we leave.

RASHID (*Disgusted*) To give Prince Feisal these few men when with a thousand times their number he could not storm the Turkish guns that face him at Medina. Is that the only purpose of this mad gallop that is killing us all?

LAWRENCE No. Not to give Feisal a few men to help him storm Medina, but to give him one who will stop him from trying to storm it at all.

RASHID Yourself? (LAWRENCE *nods*) You will not persuade him. He believes in his madness he can drive the Turkish armies from all of the Hejaz.

LAWRENCE And so do I, Rashid, and I am not mad.

RASHID By Allah, I think you are madder. How can he drive the Turks from the Hejaz and not attack their fortresses?

LAWRENCE Precisely by not attacking their fortresses, Rashid.

RASHID And so he will win his battles by not fighting them?

LAWRENCE Yes. And his war too—by not waging it.

RASHID It is a splendid riddle, el Aurans.

LAWRENCE The answer is easy, Rashid. It lies all around you. You have only to look. (*He points to the horizon*) What do you see?

RASHID Empty space.

LAWRENCE (*Pointing again*) And there—what do you see?

RASHID (*Shrugging*) Our camels.

LAWRENCE Desert and camels. Two weapons that are mightier than the mightiest guns in all the Turkish armies. The two weapons that can win Feisal his war—if only we are in time to stop him destroying his army and his own faith and courage against the guns of Medina. (*He breaks off at the sound of a shot, followed by confused shouting, coming from close at hand*) See what that is. Tell the men to save their energies for the ride, and their ammunition for the Turks. Get them mounted. (RASHID *runs off in the direction of the sound of angry voices which still continues. Pushing* HAMED *with his foot*) Leave your dreams, Hamed. It is time to go.

(HAMED *looks up at* LAWRENCE *bewildered, and then quickly jumps to his feet. He picks up* LAWRENCE'S *pistol.* LAWRENCE *takes the pistol from him and inspects it*)

LAWRENCE If this pistol could speak it would surely say: "See how my guardian reveres me. He keeps me spotless and gleaming, and ready for my master's use." (*Pause*) Is that not so, Hamed? (HAMED *makes no reply. Sighing*) May Allah give us a short war and not a long one, or your lack of conversation may grow oppressive by the end. (HAMED *looks quickly at him. Cheerfully*) Yes, Hamed. By the end. I mean to ask Prince Feisal to appoint you and Rashid permanently as my personal bodyguards. So the only way you will ever gain your freedom from my service will be to ask me for it, and without a spit to follow it. (HAMED *appears to pay no attention to news that is plainly unwelcome. He picks up a cartridge belt that* RASHID *had left behind*) He is safe, Hamed. I sent him on an errand— (*The sound of voices off grows loud again.* RASHID *runs on quickly. He looks startled*) Well?

RASHID (*Breathlessly*) Mahmoud the Moroccan has killed Salem of the Ageyli. Salem had insulted Mahmoud's tribe, and Mahmoud took his rifle and shot him when he lay asleep. Now the men of the Ageyli have bound Mahmoud and will leave him here for the vultures when we go.

LAWRENCE (*Quickly*) And the other Moroccans? Where are they?

RASHID Guarded by the Ageyli, each with a rifle to his back. They can do nothing, el Aurans. There are two Ageyli to each one of them.

LAWRENCE And the others?

RASHID They say it is no concern of theirs. Perhaps they will listen to *you*, el Aurans, but they would not hear me. (*There is a pause.* LAWRENCE *looks at the ground in thought*)

LAWRENCE (*At length, quietly*) Yes, Rashid. They must listen to me. I am their leader. (HAMED *smiles.* LAWRENCE'S *eyes meet his. Raising his voice slightly and speaking to* HAMED) They are soldiers in the field, and I lead them. If Mahmoud has committed murder then he must be killed. But— (*After evident difficulty in forcing the thought into speech*) by me—and not by them.

RASHID They will not allow that, el Aurans. The Ageyli must kill him themselves, or their honor will not be avenged.

LAWRENCE And the honor of the other Moroccans who fight for Feisal? How will that be avenged when they no longer have Ageyli rifles in their backs? You know well enough, Rashid, and so do I. And then another Moroccan will die. And another Ageyli. No. *One* life for *one* life. (*He looks at his pistol and abstractedly fingers it*) If they wish, the Moroccans can avenge *their* honor by killing me. Then it is only a Christian who dies and there will be no blood feud. (*Looking at his pistol*) Once with this I could hit a matchbox at twenty yards. I wonder now if I can kill a man at one. (*He turns to go.* RASHID *and* HAMED *make to follow him*) No. Stay here. I'll face them without a bodyguard. At least I must try to make them think I am not afraid.

(*He goes out. The lights fade. In the darkness we hear first the sound of confused shouts and cries and, at a moment, growing much louder. Then there is a quick silence, broken by a voice crying suddenly, in agonized fear:* "Have pity, el Aurans. Give me mercy. Let me live!" *Then comes a pistol shot followed at uncertain intervals by two more*)

Scene six

Scene: The lights come on to illustrate a large wall map of the Hejaz railway. It is being studied by two men, one the TURKISH GENERAL *whom we have previously seen in front of the lecturer's screen, and the other a* TURKISH CAPTAIN.

GENERAL (*Pointing at the map*) The latest report then puts him about here.

CAPTAIN Further east. Here. Nearer to Wadi Sirhan.

GENERAL But that's over a hundred miles from the railway. Are you sure that's correct?

CAPTAIN It was confirmed by our agents.

GENERAL When was his last raid on the railway?

CAPTAIN Ten days ago at kilometer 1121. (*He points to a place on the railway which is marked in kilometers*) He blew up the line in three places.

GENERAL And nothing since then?

CAPTAIN No. Perhaps our railway patrols are getting too hot for him.

GENERAL The history of the last few months would hardly

support that rather optimistic hypothesis. But why has he gone northeast away from Feisal? (*He turns away from the map. Peremptorily*) Take this down. (*The* CAPTAIN *picks up a pencil and notebook. Dictating*) Proclamation. To all loyal inhabitants of Southern Arabia. For some time past the criminal activities of a British spy, saboteur and train-wrecker, named Lawrence, sometimes known as el Aurans, Laurens Bey or the Emir Dynamite, has been causing severe damage to Arabian property, notably the Holy Railway route from Damascus to Medina. In addition, his acts of wanton destruction pose a severe threat to the supplies of our garrison at Medina. A reward, therefore, of ten thousand pounds will be paid—

CAPTAIN (*Looking up, surprised*) For a figure like that we'll need authorization from Damascus.

GENERAL I'll write to them. (*Continuing*) —will be paid to any person giving information leading to his capture. By order of the Military Governor, District of Deraa.

CAPTAIN Isn't that rather expensive for a terrorist?

GENERAL For a terrorist. But not, I think, for Lawrence.

CAPTAIN What's the difference?

GENERAL The difference between a nuisance and a menace.

CAPTAIN Menace? (*Scornfully*) The Emir Dynamite?

GENERAL (*Turning to the map*) The Emir Dynamite seems

John Mills and Paul Sparer, as LAWRENCE and AUDA ABU TAYI

to be skilled in other things than high explosives. Strategy for instance. I don't think ten thousand is too much for a man who, in a few months, has transformed a local disturbance into a major campaign—who has isolated Medina (*He points to the map*) and who has drawn down (*He points to the area of the Hejaz and Southern Arabia*) into Southern Arabia, reinforcements from all over the Turkish Empire which are needed elsewhere. (*Abstractedly*) Oh no. For this man I think ten thousand's rather cheap. (*With sudden excitement*) Nearer to the *Wadi Sirhan?* Isn't that what you said?

CAPTAIN (*At the map*) Yes. (*He points*) Here.

GENERAL But, of course. Auda!
(*The lights fade as the sound of Auda's Battle Song can be heard being sung to Arab musical accompaniment*)

Scene seven

Scene: Outside an Arab tent. The sound of a song is coming from somewhere in the distance. LAWRENCE, *in Arab clothes, is squatting on the ground with eyelids lowered.* RASHID *comes in quickly and speaks in a low voice.*

RASHID El Aurans, there is danger. (LAWRENCE *raises his head slowly, as if interrupted in some process of thought*) Hamed has just heard that the Turks have lately been to this camp and were received with great friendliness. (LAWRENCE *looks at him vaguely, his thoughts evidently elsewhere. Desperately*) El Aurans, all Arabia knows this man loves money and takes it from the Turks. Hamed says we should leave at once.

LAWRENCE Then he should come and tell me so himself.

RASHID You know well he cannot. (*Giggling*) And now he has made it even harder to break his silence to you. He has bound himself by the holiest vow he knows.

LAWRENCE Well—at least that shows he feels temptation.

RASHID Oh yes. He is tempted.

LAWRENCE Hamed's must surely be the most prolonged religious sulk in world history.

RASHID (*Urgently*) We have the camels ready, el Aurans. We can leave now.

LAWRENCE (*Quietly*) No, Rashid. Not yet. I will tell you when. (*The* SHEIK AUDA ABU TAYI *appears in the tent opening, studying a map with intense concentration. We have seen him already from the lecturer's screen, but we now see him more clearly as an old man of great vigor, with a booming voice, a handsome, hawklike face and a natural, unassumed majesty of presence. The latter quality is enhanced by the splendor of his clothes. At a nod from* LAWRENCE, RASHID *has disappeared.* AUDA *lowers the map and glares at* LAWRENCE) Well?

AUDA (*At length*) No. It is impossible.

LAWRENCE Since when has Auda Abu Tayi been turned back from any venture by the dull bonds of possibility?

AUDA El Aurans, it is only a few hours that I have known you, but I understand you better than you think I do. You have said to yourself, Auda is an old man who feeds on flattery. All I need to do to bend him to my will is to remind him of the great feats of his youth. (*Suddenly shouting*) Of course there was a time when I ignored the word impossible. There was a time, forty years ago, when I led a hundred men across the Southern Desert against ten times that number to avenge an insult to my tribe—and by the great God, avenged it too. That day I killed seven men by my own hand.

LAWRENCE Seven? In the Ballad of Auda it says ten.

AUDA (*Carelessly*) No doubt some others died of their wounds. Yes, by heaven. That feat was impossible. And there were others too— (*He changes tone*) But I am no longer twenty and what you suggest is— (*Shouting, off, angrily at someone offstage*) Kerim! Order that man, on pain of instant decapitation, to stop singing his foolish song. The words are exaggerated and his voice disturbs our thought. (*He turns back to* LAWRENCE) There is a boundary between the possible and the impossible that certain exceptional beings such as myself may leap. But there is a boundary between the impossible and a madman's dream— (*The song stops abruptly*) Thank Allah! There are fifty-six verses to that song—each in praise of either one of my battles or one of my wives. By the dispensation of God the numbers are exactly equal.

LAWRENCE Wouldn't it be supremely fitting to the memory of a great warrior if his wives were outnumbered by just one battle—and that one the greatest of all?

AUDA (*Passionately*) El Aurans, I have no great love for the Turks. Feisal is my friend and I would be his ally. But what are you asking? A march in the worst month of the year across the worst desert in Arabia—el Houl—the desolate—that even the jackals and vultures fear—where the sun can beat a man to madness and where day or night a wind of such scorching dryness can blow that a man's skin is stripped from his body. It is a terrible desert—el Houl—and terrible is not a word that comes lightly to the lips of Auda Abu Tayi.

LAWRENCE (*Mildly*) I had believed it a word unknown to him.

AUDA My friend, your flattery will not make wells. And it will not stop the few wells there *are* on the fringe of that desert from being poisoned by the Turks the moment they learn of our objective—as they must—

LAWRENCE Why must they?

AUDA Do you think I am unknown in Arabia? Do you think that when Auda rides out at the head of five hundred men the Turks will not ask questions?

LAWRENCE Indeed they will, but will they get the right answer?

AUDA They are not fools.

LAWRENCE No. And that is why the last thing they will look for is an attack across el Houl on the port of Akaba. If such a project seems mad even to Auda, how will it seem to the Turks?

AUDA (*Chuckling*) By heaven—there is some wisdom there, el Aurans. They would not even guess at it. No sane man ever could—

LAWRENCE (*Taking the map*) But just in case they do, the direction of our march should be northwest at first, to make them believe we are aiming at a raid on the railway.

AUDA (*Abstractedly interrupting*) Has Feisal much gold?

LAWRENCE Alas—he is rich only in promises—and so am I on his behalf.

AUDA And what would you have promised me if I had consented to this madness?

LAWRENCE A higher price than the Turks could pay.

AUDA Then it must be high indeed. What is it?

LAWRENCE The praise of the whole world for the most brilliant feat of arms in Arabian history.
(There is a pause)

AUDA *(Gazing at the map)* Akaba! Even your own all-powerful Navy has not dared attack it.

LAWRENCE Oh yes.

AUDA And were defeated?

LAWRENCE Oh no. Our Navy is never defeated.

AUDA Well?

LAWRENCE After a successful bombardment they withdrew.

AUDA Beaten off by the Turkish guns.

LAWRENCE They are very powerful guns.

AUDA Have *I* powerful guns?

LAWRENCE You have no need of guns.

AUDA How? No need?

LAWRENCE There is no gun—however powerful—that can fire backwards.
(*There is a pause*)

AUDA They all point out to sea?

LAWRENCE All out to sea.

AUDA Fixed?

LAWRENCE Fixed.
(*Another pause*)

AUDA How strong are the Turks?

LAWRENCE About two thousand in the area.

AUDA Against five hundred?

LAWRENCE Four to one. Auda's odds.

AUDA (*Chuckling*) Auda's odds. Have they made no preparations against an attack from the land?

LAWRENCE None.

AUDA They believe it impossible?

LAWRENCE A madman's dream.

AUDA (*Chuckling*) The fools. No fortifications facing the land at all?

LAWRENCE A few—a very few—but they will be easy to surprise.

AUDA A camel charge, at night. My battle cry, to panic the idiots from their beds, and then amongst them.

LAWRENCE They may well surrender at the very sound.

AUDA (*Genuinely alarmed*) May Allah forbid! My friend, do you think I am marching across el Houl in the deadliest month of the year, to be rewarded at the end with a tame surrender?

LAWRENCE Well—then—perhaps no battle cry—

AUDA That, too, is unthinkable. Even Turks must know who it is that kills them. A charge in daylight, then—after due warning—

LAWRENCE Not too long a warning.

AUDA Not too long and not too short. Akaba! What a gift to make to Feisal—

TURKISH CAPTAIN (*Off*) Keep the men mounted—
(*The* TURKISH CAPTAIN *walks in, past* LAWRENCE *without glancing at him, and up to* AUDA *who has turned at his tent opening. He salutes*)

CAPTAIN God be with you, Auda Abu Tayi!

AUDA And with you, Captain.

(LAWRENCE *moves unobtrusively to go, but finds his escape barred by a* TURKISH SOLDIER, *whose back can be seen as he lounges at the entrance.* LAWRENCE *slips to the ground adopting the same squatting attitude in which we first saw him in this scene. He keeps his head lowered*)

CAPTAIN I bring the greetings and love of my master, the Governor, and the precious gift for which you asked— (*He holds out a small package.* AUDA *snatches it eagerly*)

AUDA By God, but this has been fast work—

CAPTAIN His Excellency telegraphed to Damascus and had it sent down by the railway.

AUDA Ah—this is a noble sight— (*He reveals the contents of the package with a delighted flourish. They are a set of false teeth*) By Allah, these are surely the false teeth of which all other false teeth are but vile and blaspheming copies. Your master's generous answer to his servant's dire need is a great and splendid thing, and will not be forgotten—

CAPTAIN I shall tell him of your pleasure—it will add to his own.

AUDA See how well they are made, and how they gleam in the sun. By the prophet, with these in my mouth, I shall be young again. You must eat with me tonight, Captain—and you shall see them in action—

CAPTAIN I am afraid that will not be possible. I must start back at once.

AUDA (*Still admiring the teeth*) A pity. You must ask your master what gift he would like from me in return—

CAPTAIN You know the gift.

AUDA Ah yes, I remember— (*He puts the teeth back in the package a trifle abstractedly*) Why are you so sure he will come to me?

CAPTAIN The Governor believes that he'll try to win you to the rebel cause.

AUDA That would be very foolish.

CAPTAIN Let us hope he is so foolish, Auda. I know my master would rather you earned the reward than anyone.

AUDA (*Interested*) Reward? You said nothing before of a reward.

CAPTAIN It had not then been authorized.

AUDA (*Abstractedly*) How much?

CAPTAIN Ten thousand pounds.

AUDA (*With a gasp*) Ten thousand! By Allah—is this Englishman worth so much?

CAPTAIN The Governor believes him to be.

AUDA Ten thousand. (*Suddenly speaking to* LAWRENCE'S

lowered head) Do you hear that, my friend?
(Pause. LAWRENCE *slowly raises his head)*

LAWRENCE *(Looking up at him)* Yes, Auda. I hear it.

AUDA What do you say?

LAWRENCE That it is indeed a high price for so low a scoundrel.

AUDA It is indeed a high price. A very high price. Would you like to see me win it?

LAWRENCE I would rather win it, myself. But if not I, then let it be you. For surely no reward is too great for Auda Abu Tayi.
(Pause. The CAPTAIN *has glanced at* LAWRENCE *with only mild interest.* AUDA *turns back to him)*

AUDA He speaks loyally and well.

CAPTAIN He does. *(Reassuringly)* We have no fears, Auda. We know that you and all the men about you are loyal. But *you* must fear this Englishman. He has a glib and flattering tongue and by it has lured good men into treachery.

AUDA Below medium height?

CAPTAIN Yes.

AUDA And dresses usually in white?

CAPTAIN So it is said.

AUDA Looking more English than Arab?

CAPTAIN Yes. But you won't need to recognize him, Auda. He will surely announce himself to you. And then—

AUDA And then?

CAPTAIN You know what to do to gain ten thousand pounds.

AUDA Yes. I know what to do.

CAPTAIN I shall give your messages to the Governor.

AUDA (*To* LAWRENCE, *abruptly*) Escort the Captain—
(LAWRENCE *gets to his feet*)

CAPTAIN Thank you, but there is no need—

AUDA Do you think we have no manners here?

CAPTAIN (*Smiling*) God be with you, Auda.

AUDA And with you, Captain.

CAPTAIN (*To* LAWRENCE, *who has stationed himself behind him*) Oh, thank you—
(*He goes out.* AUDA *moves quickly to look after him, looking tense and anxious. We hear the sound of a barked*

word of command, and of horses' hooves moving away. AUDA *relaxes and shrugs his shoulders.* LAWRENCE *comes back)*

AUDA By heaven, el Aurans, what a joke that was! What a joke to remember—

LAWRENCE (*In a low, uncertain voice*) It won't be easy to forget.

AUDA (*Touching his arm*) My friend, you are trembling.

LAWRENCE Yes. I am.

AUDA You were afraid?

LAWRENCE Yes.

AUDA Of what? Of a degenerate Turk and his few followers? There are five hundred men in this camp. They could have accounted for them in twenty seconds.

LAWRENCE Yes. They could. The question is whether they would.

AUDA By Allah, they would if I had ordered them.

LAWRENCE Yes. But would you have ordered them?

AUDA Can you doubt it?

LAWRENCE With some ease.

AUDA But, my friend, if I had wanted the reward—

LAWRENCE Auda, do you believe your thoughts are so hard to read? To betray a guest is a great sin, but ten thousand pounds is ten thousand pounds, and surely worth a spin of the wheel of fate. If the Turk recognizes the foreigner, then the foreigner is not betrayed. But, to be recognized, he must first be made to raise his head and show the Turk his English features and then to stand up to show the Turk his white clothes and his meager height—

AUDA (*Chuckling*) What a fool he was, that Turk! (*To* LAWRENCE) Of course I knew he was a fool or I would never have taken that risk. (LAWRENCE *looks at him, without replying. Moving to the tent*) Come, my friend. We have plans to make. (LAWRENCE *makes no move to follow him*) Very well. I admit that I was tempted. You offered me honor and they, money. Both I love exceedingly and not the one much more than the other. But I spun the wheel and honor won. There is no going back now.

LAWRENCE And if they raised my price?

AUDA Ah. But they will not raise your price until after we have taken Akaba. (LAWRENCE *smiles, shrugs his shoulders and goes slowly towards the tent opening.* AUDA *has picked up the package and is looking at his precious false teeth. Suddenly he hurls them to the ground, picks up a rifle and smashes the butt on them, again and again. After a moment he stops, stoops and picks up the shattered frag-*

ments, looking at them with eyes of tragic longing. Then he throws them carelessly away) The path of honor.

(He puts his arm round LAWRENCE *and escorts him into the tent. The lights fade. In the darkness we hear the sound of "Tipperary" played on a rather scratchy record.*

Scene eight

Scene: A small hut in a British Army camp near Suez. As the lights come on they focus first on an ancient gramophone, complete with horn. A man is humming the song to this accompaniment and, as the lights come up more strongly, we see he is a BRITISH CORPORAL *and is using a disinfectant spray in time to the music. The camp has been abandoned through an outbreak of plague, and the hut bears a dilapidated appearance. A door is open at the back, showing the night sky.* HAMED, *looking ragged and desert-stained, comes into the hut and looks around.*

CORPORAL (*Gesticulating*) Yellah! Yellah! Shoo! (HAMED *pays no attention, but walks over to a desk where he has seen a telephone*) Get out of here, woggie. Go on. Hop it, now— (HAMED *picks up the receiver gingerly—rather as if he expected from it some kind of electric shock*) Get out, woggie, or I'll have to shoot you, and you wouldn't like that, now, would you? This is British Army property and I'm in charge—see. Shoo! Yellah! Shoo! (HAMED, *still paying no attention to the* CORPORAL, *lifts the receiver rather fearfully to his ear, still evidently expecting to be electrocuted. Reassured by his immunity he listens for a moment, until a voice can be heard asking for a number. Meanwhile*) Shoo, shoo, shoo, shoo! Out, woggie, out! (HAMED, *still paying no attention to the* CORPORAL *but satisfied, apparently, with what he has heard on the telephone, re-*

places the receiver and walks out. The CORPORAL, *after a shrug, continues his fumigating. The record comes to an end. He is bending over the gramophone as* LAWRENCE *comes in. He looks as travel-stained and dirty as* HAMED) Cripes! Another one. (*Shouting*) Yellah! Yellah! Yellah! Shoo! (*He uses his spray on* LAWRENCE) Get to hell out of here, woggie! I nearly shot your chum and I'll shoot you, I swear, if you don't buzz off!

LAWRENCE (*At telephone*) Does this telephone work, Corporal?

CORPORAL (*At length*) Did you speak?

LAWRENCE Yes, I asked if this telephone works. I want to ring up Suez—

CORPORAL (*Beyond his depth*) I am in charge of this camp, which is Government property, and which has been closed down on account of plague—and no unauthorized person may—

LAWRENCE (*Into telephone*) Naval Headquarters. It's urgent. (*To* CORPORAL) Ah. Plague. So that explains it. For the last half hour I've been wondering if the British troops on the Suez Canal had got bored with the war and gone home.

CORPORAL (*Pointing to telephone*) Listen—I said no unauthorized person—

LAWRENCE (*Into receiver*) Hullo, Naval Headquarters? I

want your senior chap, whoever he is . . . Admiral Makepeace? Right. Put me through . . . No. I don't want any duty officer. I want the man in charge. . . . Then get him away from dinner. . . . Then you'll have to forget your orders, won't you? . . . My name will mean nothing to you and my rank is unimportant, but I can only tell you that if you fail to get your Admiral to the telephone this instant you will probably face a court-martial for having delayed the ending of the war by roughly three months . . . I see. Just hold on a moment . . . (*He puts his hand over the receiver and turns to the* CORPORAL) Get me some water from that tap outside, would you, old chap?

CORPORAL It's not for drinking. Strict orders are to boil all water—

LAWRENCE The last well I drank from—yesterday morning —had a dead goat in it.

CORPORAL Yes—er—sir. As you say.
(*He goes*)

LAWRENCE (*Into the telephone, mildly*) Now, in answer to your question, I am not off my bleeding chump. I am speaking the simple truth. At your switchboard you hold in your hands the lives of five hundred Allied soldiers and the possession of the most valuable port in Southern Arabia, in which at the moment those soldiers are victoriously sitting, with nothing whatever to eat except their camels or their prisoners, and if I know them, they'll start on the prisoners. . . . Thank you. (*The* CORPORAL *has come back with a mug of water.* LAWRENCE *takes it from him)* By jove, Corporal, it's worked. I think he still thinks I'm off my rocker, though—

CORPORAL *(Politely)* Does he, sir? Fancy.

*(*LAWRENCE *splutters into the mug from which he is avidly drinking. After a moment he puts it down)*

LAWRENCE I've got some men outside who need food and drink. Would you look after them?

CORPORAL Yes, sir. I don't speak their lingo, sir.

LAWRENCE If you smile at them and treat them as if they were human, you'll find them quite easy to handle—

CORPORAL Yes, sir. I'll do my best.

(He goes out)

LAWRENCE *(Into telephone)* Oh, hullo, Admiral. Sorry to disturb you . . . My name's Lawrence, Captain Lawrence . . . Oh, no. Just Army. Look. I want you to send a destroyer to Akaba . . . Destroyer, that's right, but it doesn't *have* to be a destroyer. As a matter of fact a bigger thing —might be better. It's got to take a lot of stuff, you see— food for five hundred men, about six howitzers, thirty machine guns, as many grenades and rifles as the Army will let you have—oh—and some armored cars would come in very handy. Also—most important of all really— about fifty thousand pounds in cash . . . Fifty thousand . . . Oh, I'm sorry. Didn't I tell you. . . . Yes, we took it. . . . From the land. Rather a long way round, but it seemed to work all right. . . . No. They didn't appear to expect us . . . Oh, about five hundred killed and seven hundred prisoners. . . . Ours? Two. Unhappily we lost five more on the march, including one of my bodyguards. You see conditions in the desert were a bit—rough. We had three bad sandstorms, and I'm afraid my compass work wasn't all that good, and we missed a well— . . . No, Admiral, I promise you this isn't a joke. Akaba is ours . . . A rather picturesque fellow called Auda Abu Tayi is holding it, but don't let him sell it to you, because he'll certainly try. Now you will get that boat there tonight, won't you? You see, the Turks are bound to react violently, and mount a counteroffensive in the next few days. Will you please inform Cairo for me? I'm a bit tired . . . No. I won't be available tomorrow. I shall be asleep tomorrow and probably the next day. If they want to talk to me after that they'll find me in my old office in Cairo . . . Making maps . . . Yes. The C-in-C does know of me. In fact, General Murray and I have often exchanged words . . . Gone? Gone for good? (*Plainly delighted*) Oh dear! Who, then . . . Allenby? No. I've not heard of him. Thank you, sir. Goodnight. (*He rings off and rests his head on the desk.* HAMED *stalks angrily into the office, holding a sausage on a fork, keeping it as far away from him as possible.* LAWRENCE *looks up*) Yes, Hamed? (HAMED *thrusts the fork angrily at him.* LAWRENCE *takes it*) Ah, I see. The infidel Corporal has not understood the laws of Allah. You must forgive him. (*He pulls the sausage from the fork and begins to eat it*) Avert your pious eyes from your master's vile gluttony, Hamed, and remember that he has not eaten since yesterday's dawn. Remember too that it was to the Faithful that he gave up his rations. (HAMED *lowers his eyes.* LAWRENCE *looks up at him, wearily, without getting up. Smiling)* Since Rashid died I have not seen you smile, Hamed. Not once. But before you had begun to learn the trick. (*Quietly*) Tell me. Is it that you blame me? (HAMED *signifies dissent*) You can tell me if it is true. I shall understand. (HAMED *again signifies dissent*) You smile, then, at no one? At nothing? (HAMED *signifies agreement*) Because of your grief, and only because of that? (HAMED *signifies assent*) I am sorry, Hamed. If there was anything that I could have found to say to you that might have helped you, I would have found it. But I will not insult you by trying to tell you that one day you will forget. I know as well as you that you will not. But, at least, in time you will not remember as fiercely as you do now—and I pray that that time may be soon. I shall see that the corporal gives you food more fitting to Moslem warriors. I want anyway to say goodbye to you all—

(*He gets up showing his utter exhaustion. His back is turned to us as* HAMED *speaks*)

HAMED (*With certainty*) You will come back to us, el Aurans.

(LAWRENCE *turns slowly to look at him. There is a long pause*)

LAWRENCE Others will come, Hamed. Many others of my countrymen. That is certain.

HAMED There are no others we need, but you. (*There is a pause. The telephone rings.* LAWRENCE *makes no move to pick up the receiver*) You must come back to us, el Aurans. It is you that we need.

LAWRENCE (*Finally picking up receiver*) Yes . . . Yes, this is Lawrence . . . Who? Flag Lieutenant? Hold on a moment. (*He lowers the receiver*) Go to the men, Hamed. I'll join you there. (HAMED *turns to go*) And Hamed. (HAMED *turns*) Thank you for your words. Any words from you would have been welcome, but those words more welcome than all. (HAMED *goes. Into receiver*) I'm sorry . . . To get across the Canal? Well, I thought I'd get some fellow to row me . . . The Admiral's barge? I say, how splendid. Thank you. (*He rings off. Sitting at the desk he suddenly raises his head in fierce and glowing pride. Softly*) Ross, can you hear me? (*Pause*) I've done it. Done it. I've captured Akaba. I've done what none of the professional soldiers could have done. I've captured the key to Southern Arabia with five hundred inefficient, untrustworthy Arab bandits. Why don't you enjoy the memory? What makes you so unhappy? Is it that Moroccan I shot in the desert and couldn't kill cleanly because my hand was shaking so much? The mangled Turkish bodies in the dynamited trains? Those men that died in the desert? . . . Rashid? . . . Is it Rashid? (*Pause*) War is war, after all. The enemy has to be killed and our own men have to die. And surely, at least I've been more sparing of them than any red-tabbed superman? (*Pause. Angrily*) What is wrong in trying to write my name in history? Lawrence of Akaba—perhaps—who knows? (*Pause*) Oh, Ross—how did I become you?

(*He gets up and goes wearily out of the hut*)

Curtain

ACT TWO

ACT TWO

Scene one

Scene: A room in G.H.Q., Cairo. There is an imposing desk, a large wall map, and comfortable armchairs; behind the desk sits ALLENBY, *a large, heavy man, his appearance rather belying his character.*

A very decorative A.D.C. *steps smartly into the room and comes to parade-ground attention.*

ALLENBY Are they here?

A.D.C. Yes, sir.

ALLENBY Show them in. (*The* A.D.C. *turns and goes out. After a moment* STORRS *and* BARRINGTON *come in*) Good morning, Colonel. Ah, Storrs—good of you to come.

STORRS Not at all, sir. Even in my lax office a request from the Commander-in-Chief is usually counted as an order.

ALLENBY (*Not smiling*) Sit down, gentlemen, please. (*They do so*) I've called you here because I understand you both know this fellow Lawrence. (*They signify assent*) I don't want to hear too much of what you think of him as a man. I'm prepared to form my own judgment on that. I'm seeing him later on. I want you to tell me what you think of him as a potential leader. Storrs?

STORRS Lawrence as a leader? (*Thoughtfully*) He's pure intellectual, and not by nature a man of action at all. He's strongly introverted, withdrawn and self-conscious, and will never allow anyone to see his true nature. He hides everything behind a manner that's either overmeek, overarrogant, or overflippant, whichever is going to disconcert the most. He thinks far too much for the good of his soul and feels far too much for the good of his mind. Consequently he's a highly unstable personality. Finally, he has a sublime contempt for authority—in any form, but chiefly military.

ALLENBY I see. Not very promising—

STORRS On the contrary, sir. I think he'd make a military leader of the highest class.

ALLENBY (*Snapping*) Why?

STORRS Because I find to my surprise that I've just given a description of most great commanders from Julius Caesar to Napoleon.

ALLENBY (*Nodding after a moment*) Barrington?

BARRINGTON I disagree, sir, I'm afraid. I don't deny his success in Akaba—though how much luck there was in that, we'll never know. (*Angrily*) But give him all credit for Akaba—it still makes no difference. He's irresponsible—a useful man, no doubt, to have charging around behind the enemy lines with his Bedouins blowing up trains. But in a position of responsibility—no. Definitely, no. May I ask, sir, what appointment you had in mind?

ALLENBY In a report to me he has recommended a plan for general revolt of all the Arab peoples in the north—to be timed to coincide with my offensive through the Gaza Gap in November. (*To* BARRINGTON) By the way, security must be dangerously bad here for him to have known both the time and the place of my offensive.

BARRINGTON On the contrary, sir, security here is very good. I didn't know either time or place and I'm sure Storrs didn't—did you?

STORRS No.

ALLENBY Well, then, how on earth did *he?*
(*There is a pause*)

STORRS (*Mildly*) A point to me, I think.

BARRINGTON Guesswork.

STORRS One of the qualities of a leader, isn't it?

ALLENBY Possibly. Still, I wish he'd confine his attention to the enemy's plans, and not to mine. However, he suggests that, to support my offensive, four separate Arab forces should be organized to operate east of the Hejaz railway, between Maan and Damascus here— (*He points*) along the Turks' main line of communication—
(*A pause*)

BARRINGTON (*Ironically, at length*) A rather ambitious plan, isn't it?

ALLENBY (*Shortly*) Highly, but I'm accepting it. In fact, I'm accepting all his recommendations, except one—that a high-ranking officer be appointed to direct these operations. I'm thinking of appointing Lawrence himself.

BARRINGTON (*Pained*) A Captain?

ALLENBY He was gazetted Major this morning. And I've recommended him for an award.

BARRINGTON I'm afraid my opinion must remain that it would be a very dangerous appointment. Forgive my frankness, sir.

ALLENBY (*Dryly*) It does you credit. Storrs?

STORRS I'll stick to my opinion too.

ALLENBY (*Presses a bell on his desk*) I'm grateful to you both. (*The* A.D.C. *appears*) Is Major Lawrence here?

A.D.C. He's just arrived, sir.

ALLENBY Send him in. (*The* A.D.C. *goes. To* STORRS) I'm a bit scared of this meeting. Do you think he'll try to floor me with Baudelaire or something?

STORRS Very likely, sir.

ALLENBY I wonder if I could floor him with my pet subject.

BARRINGTON What's that, sir?

ALLENBY Flowers.

(BARRINGTON *looks startled. A door is opened and* LAWRENCE *comes in. He is dressed in a uniform that was never from Savile Row, but now—after loss of weight in the desert—hardly fits him at all. He sees* STORRS *first*)

LAWRENCE Oh, hullo, Storrs. I was coming to see you this aft— (*A firm sign from* STORRS *indicates the Commander-in-Chief*) Oh, I'm sorry.

(*He delivers a rather informal-looking salute. Even* ALLENBY, *determined to be surprised at nothing, has to comment*)

ALLENBY Good gracious!

LAWRENCE What's the matter?

ALLENBY Do you always salute like that?

LAWRENCE Why, sir? Is it wrong?

ALLENBY It's a little—individual.

LAWRENCE I was never taught.

ALLENBY But you must have done some drill training, surely?

LAWRENCE Well, no. I was a civilian in the Map Section of the War Office in 1914 and one of my jobs was to take maps along to some old General—and he always used to roar at me that he hated civilians in his office and why the dickens wasn't I in uniform? So, one day, I went out to the Army and Navy Stores and bought a uniform.

ALLENBY (*Unsmiling*) You mean that you've never been properly commissioned in the Army?

LAWRENCE I don't think so, sir. No. I'm sure I'd remember it if I had.

ALLENBY I see. Well, I'm happy to inform you that you've now been gazetted a Major.

LAWRENCE (*Mildly*) Oh? Good.

ALLENBY And I've put in a recommendation for you for the C.B.

LAWRENCE (*Startled*) C.B.?

ALLENBY Companion of the Bath.

LAWRENCE Oh. Thank you.

ALLENBY (*To the other two*) Very well, gentlemen. Thank you very much.
(*They turn to go*)

LAWRENCE Oh, Storrs. (*To* ALLENBY) Excuse me. (ALLENBY *nods*) Freddie Strong has dug up something at Luxor which I know you'll go absolutely mad about.

(STORRS, *detained at the door, is looking acutely embarrassed.* BARRINGTON *flashes* ALLENBY *his parade-ground salute and goes, his face meaningful. Apparently oblivious*) It's a small alabaster perfume jar, exquisite shape, twentieth dynasty I should think, with what seems like a strong Minoan influence—

ALLENBY (*Quietly*) Minoan influence in the twentieth dynasty?
(LAWRENCE *turns to look at him, apparently seeing him for the first time*)

LAWRENCE (*At length*) I suppose it couldn't be, could it? I must have got the dynasty wrong.

ALLENBY Or the influence.

LAWRENCE (*Slowly*) Yes. Or the influence.

ALLENBY (*With authority*) Goodbye, Storrs, and thank you.

STORRS Goodbye, sir.
(*He goes with evident relief*)

ALLENBY Sit down, Lawrence. (LAWRENCE *sits. There is a pause. Smiling suddenly*) Tell me—did Freddie Strong really dig up a twentieth-dynasty perfume jar?
(*There is a pause while* LAWRENCE *and* ALLENBY *look at each other appraisingly across the large desk*)

LAWRENCE (*At length—with a good-humored shrug*) Well, he does dig things up all the time, you know.

ALLENBY (*Nodding appreciatively*) Good. I'm glad we understand each other so soon.

LAWRENCE (*Without rancor*) Yes. So am I.

ALLENBY I was lucky with the Minoan influence. I've just been reading Arthur Evans' book, *The Palace of Minos in Crete.*

LAWRENCE (*Politely*) It's pleasant to meet a General who's read anything except Clausewitz.

ALLENBY Yes. You won't catch me on Clausewitz, although I confess I'm a bit rusty. But please don't try me on the campaigns of Belisarius. I gather that *is* one of your pet subjects?

LAWRENCE Yes. How did you know?

ALLENBY I've made it my business to find out. No doubt you've done the same about me.

LAWRENCE Flowers?

ALLENBY Correct.

LAWRENCE Shakespeare, Chippendale, mobile warfare, Chopin and children. Not, of course, necessarily, in that order.

ALLENBY Your spies have done even better than mine.

LAWRENCE I expect yours had less to find out.

ALLENBY More, I think—but your talent for self-concealment is greater.

LAWRENCE Perhaps it needs to be.

ALLENBY Perhaps.

LAWRENCE (*Smiling*) A lesser man would have said: "Oh no—I'm sure not."

ALLENBY I'm not interested in the secrets of your soul, Lawrence. I'm interested in only one thing. Are you the right man for the job?

LAWRENCE (*Genuinely puzzled*) What job?

ALLENBY (*Impatiently holding up Lawrence's report and tapping it*) This, of course.

LAWRENCE (*Still puzzled*) My report? (*He gets up, evidently really disturbed*) Oh no. Great heavens, no. Not me. That would be disastrous.
(*He is plainly agitated.* ALLENBY *looks at him inquiringly, evidently wondering whether this is not just another trick*)

ALLENBY You echo Colonel Barrington.

LAWRENCE Even Colonel Barrington can be right once in a war's duration. He is now.

ALLENBY You surprise me.

LAWRENCE Why?

ALLENBY I thought you were an ambitious man.

LAWRENCE So I am.

ALLENBY Well, here might be your chance.

LAWRENCE (*Shaking his head*) I've had my chance. Akaba and being made a Major, and the—what's the thing—C.B.—that's enough, isn't it?

ALLENBY (*Thoughtfully*) I wouldn't have thought so—for you. When you were writing this report, did it never occur to you I might consider *you* for the job?

LAWRENCE Of course it did. That's why I was so determined to make it plain exactly what qualities your man would need. He must be a man of authority, with the patience to remain cheerful in the face of incompetence, cowardice, greed and treachery. He must have a deep practical knowledge of strategy, and of the principles of irregular warfare. Above all he must know how to lie and flatter and cheat in a cause that is not his own, but in which he must appear to believe. And he must forget that he's ever heard of the Sykes-Picot Agreement.

ALLENBY What agreement?

LAWRENCE (*Impatiently*) The secret treaty partitioning postwar Arabia between the French and us.

ALLENBY I've never heard of it.

LAWRENCE No? Nor, for the moment, has Feisal, but if he finds out there'll be hell to pay. So it's vital that he and his people should continually be fed, from now on, the right kind of lies by the right kind of liar. Therefore this man of yours has to be a very senior officer. Then his lies will have real weight.

ALLENBY I thought you didn't approve of senior officers.

LAWRENCE I don't approve of the man I've just described. And nor, I suspect, do you. But it's the man you want for the job. Not me, General.

ALLENBY Possibly. The difficulty is that another man hasn't already operated successfully for months behind the Turkish lines, hasn't already won the trust of the Arab rebels, and hasn't taken Akaba.

LAWRENCE What does Akaba prove?

ALLENBY Enough.

LAWRENCE Do you know why I took Akaba? Do you know why I went off alone into the desert in the first place?

ALLENBY Escape from an office?

LAWRENCE A little true.

ALLENBY Escape from yourself?

LAWRENCE I'm a Greek scholar. I have a profound belief in the virtues of self-knowledge.

ALLENBY A man can have a belief without practicing it.

LAWRENCE (*Appreciatively*) I grant you the point. Escape from myself then. What else?

ALLENBY Escape from too much thinking?

LAWRENCE No. You can't escape from that, even in the desert.

ALLENBY But the desert is a cleaner place to think in than an office.

LAWRENCE There's nothing clean or dirty but thinking makes it so. And death is dirty, even in the desert. Still, I grant you the point.

ALLENBY Finally, a burning desire to show off to my predecessor, General Murray?

LAWRENCE Also true. (*Admiringly*) I must say you've done pretty well, so far.

ALLENBY Thank you. (*Politely*) Well, now, shall we get back to the business on hand?

LAWRENCE (*Sadly*) This *is* the business on hand, I'm afraid. You've diagnosed my motives for Akaba and the rest of it quite accurately—although you left out the most important one of all—a cold-blooded experiment with will-power—but at least you must admit that all these motives have one thing in common. They're all flagrantly selfish.

ALLENBY Possibly. Does that matter?

LAWRENCE This job is for a Messiah. For a visionary with real faith—not for an intellectual misfit.

ALLENBY (*Offhandedly*) But you like the Arabs, don't you?

LAWRENCE It's not enough to like them. Your man must believe in them and their destiny.

ALLENBY What about your own country and *its* destiny?

LAWRENCE (*Quietly*) Oh yes. I believe in that. And I grant you that in war my country has a perfect right to demand my life. I doubt if it has the right to demand more.

ALLENBY Aren't you exaggerating the demands of this job a bit?

LAWRENCE (*Simply*) No. You're a trained commander, you see. When you send men out to die, you don't question whether it's *right*—only whether it's *wise*. If it's unwise, it's wrong, and only then your conscience pricks. My conscience isn't Sandhurst trained. It's as undrilled as my salute, and so soft it must have the armor-plating of a cause to believe in. (*After a pause*) How on earth can one *think* oneself into a belief?
(*There is another pause*)

ALLENBY (*Again offhandedly*) I suppose one can't. But mightn't it be possible to *will* oneself into it?
(*A pause*)

LAWRENCE (*Laughing*) You're a bit of a Mephisto, aren't you?

ALLENBY I'm flattered to be thought so.

LAWRENCE Do you know, General—I think you and I might get along very well.

ALLENBY I'm sure I hope so, Major.
(*Pause*)

LAWRENCE Well, the first thing will be money.

ALLENBY How much?

LAWRENCE The Turks are lavish spenders and we shall have to outbid them. Say two hundred thousand.

ALLENBY (*Doubtfully*) Hm.

LAWRENCE (*Cheerfully*) Thinking of the Treasury? Put it under the head of propaganda. They'll like that. It's fashionable. I shall want it all in gold, of course. The Arabs distrust bits of paper. (*Turning to the map*) Akaba must be made the main Arab base, instead of Jeddah; and I suggest you put Colonel Joyce in charge of it.

ALLENBY What about Colonel Barrington?

LAWRENCE Oh, put him on somebody's staff. Make him a General, I'm sure he's overdue. Now the most important thing of all, and this you *must* do—

ALLENBY (*Mildly*) One moment, Major Lawrence. I think I must remind you that I have not yet offered you this appointment.

LAWRENCE No. Nor you have. And I haven't accepted it yet either. Still, I might as well give you my views—don't you think—as I'm here. So—proceeding—Feisal must be detached from the forces of the Sherif of Mecca and made Commander-in-Chief of all Arab forces in the field, under the orders of yourself. And—for reasons purely of prestige —a small regular Arab force must be formed and trained to operate frontally at the decisive moment—but, of course, our main and vital effort will continue to lie in irregular operations behind the enemy lines. (*After a moment*) I think that's all.

ALLENBY Good.

LAWRENCE Well. I'd better not take up any more of your time, General. I'm sure you've got a host of important things to do. So I'll be off now, if that's all right.

ALLENBY That's all right.

LAWRENCE I've got a few things to turn over in my mind, too. By the way, some time you must convert me about Chippendale. I've always thought he was overrated. But I'm rather a Philistine about furniture. I don't use it much, you see. (*At the door*) Well, goodbye, sir.

ALLENBY Goodbye.

LAWRENCE And I suppose I shall hear from you?

ALLENBY Yes. You'll hear from me. (LAWRENCE *flashes a smile of farewell, turns to the door, and then turns back, having evidently forgotten something. He produces his eccentric salute*) One of these days I really must show you how to do that.

LAWRENCE Yes, sir, when we both have the time.
(*He goes out. The lights fade*)

SCENE TWO

A spotlight comes on gradually to illumine the face of the TURKISH GENERAL. *He is speaking into the mouthpiece of a dictaphone.*

GENERAL Circular telegram to all centers of Turkish Military Intelligence, Central Arabia. Most secret. Begins. Despite all our endeavors and the raising of the reward for Lawrence's capture to the unprecedented sum of twenty thousand pounds, he remains at large, operating behind our lines. (*The lights have come on to show the room in which the* GENERAL *sits, or rather reclines, for he is on a divan, leaning against pillows. It is a small sitting room with two doors, one leading to his bedroom, the other to the stairs. The* TURKISH CAPTAIN *sits in an armchair in a carelessly informal attitude, looking at an illustrated magazine*) The elimination of this terrorist has now become of vital concern, not only to the success of our military operations, but to the very continuance of our dominion in Arabia.

CAPTAIN You're making him sound too important. You don't want to start a panic, do you?

GENERAL (*Mildly*) Don't interrupt. Read your magazine. (*Into mouthpiece*) Since his return to Arabia six months ago Lawrence has been known to have contacted secret revolutionary groups in places as far apart as Jerusalem, Damascus and Beirut. At present he is reported to be operating in the district of Deraa itself. His aim is, probably, to start a general uprising against us, timed to coincide with a British offensive in Palestine. Meanwhile he continues his guerilla activities against our lines of communication. All this poses a threat that must on no account be taken lightly.

CAPTAIN (*Angrily*) Can you see them taking it lightly? They already think he has supernatural powers.

GENERAL (*Into mouthpiece*) Paragraph Two. Certain additional facts on Lawrence have now come to light. One. Despite rumors to the contrary he does not wear female disguise. The recent practice of forcible unveiling of women will therefore cease, as injurious to civilian good will. Two. The description of Lawrence as already circulated is accurate and has been vouched for (*With a look at the* CAPTAIN) by an officer of my staff, who once came into close contact with him.
(*The* CAPTAIN *has jumped up*)

CAPTAIN Delete that.

GENERAL (*Mildly*) I wasn't going to say which member of my staff.

CAPTAIN You would if Constantinople asked.

GENERAL I will if you don't sit down and keep quiet. (*Into mouthpiece*) Three. In view of information recently come to hand regarding Lawrence's sexual proclivities, the watch at present being maintained on brothels and similar places may be discontinued—

CAPTAIN (*Eagerly*) That's interesting. What information?

GENERAL I'm sorry to disappoint you. The information was decisively negative.

CAPTAIN In every way? (*The* GENERAL *nods*) That doesn't seem likely to me.

GENERAL (*Genially*) I'm sure it doesn't, but ascetics do exist, you know.

CAPTAIN But no one is born an ascetic. Is Lawrence very religious?

GENERAL His self-denial is self-imposed. It has also a very revealing aspect.

CAPTAIN What?

GENERAL He avoids physical contact of any kind. Even shaking hands requires an effort.

CAPTAIN I can't see what's so revealing about that—

GENERAL Can't you. (*Into mouthpiece*) Paragraph Four—

CAPTAIN (*Sulkily*) What does it reveal?

GENERAL (*Patiently*) A rebellious body, a strong will and a troubled spirit. May I go on?

CAPTAIN You mean he'd like to, but won't admit he'd like to, and so he doesn't?

GENERAL You put it very subtly. (*Into mouthpiece*) Paragraph Four. Most important. It must be brought to the attention of all personnel that the capture of Lawrence alive should now be their primary objective. When captured the criminal will not be interrogated locally, but will be handed over forthwith to the requisite high authority. By Order Military Governor, District of Deraa. Message ends. (*He puts down the mouthpiece and goes over to the table where he pours himself out a glass of wine. The* CAPTAIN *watches him disapproving*) A real French Burgundy. Have some? (*The* CAPTAIN *shakes his head*) You're such a good boy. (*Examining the glass*) I'm so glad I'm not a Christian. In their religion this isn't a sin—

CAPTAIN If I capture Lawrence, I shall shoot the swine.

GENERAL (*Mildly*) You really are very foolish, aren't you. Your bullet might well lose us Arabia. Can't you see that the man's death, by itself, would solve nothing? The Arabs would go on believing in this myth that he's taught them, Arabia for the Arabs—one race, one land, one nation. For a thousand years out here before he came, that idea was only the harmless dream of a few religious fanatics. But he's shown them the way to turn it into fact. Only half a fact as yet, Allah be praised, but even that half is a grave danger to our Empire. The whole fact? Well, then the world is in danger.

CAPTAIN (*Carelessly*) The world can sleep easily, I think.

GENERAL (*Gravely*) Feisal has chosen Damascus as his capital. (*The* CAPTAIN *laughs*) I'd laugh too if I didn't know that the brain that planted that fantasy is as brilliant, ice-cold and ruthless as any revolutionary's in history. Do you really think that a bullet in that brain will turn the Arabs back now?

CAPTAIN (*Shrugging*) What will?
(*Pause. The* GENERAL *sips his wine*)

GENERAL Well, I suppose that what a brain can create, the same brain can destroy.

CAPTAIN Get him to recant, you mean?

GENERAL It's the traditional method of dealing with heresy.

CAPTAIN But how do you do it?

GENERAL (*Shrugging*) By persuasion, I suppose. (*Looking at him*) What a pity about this climate. It ruins a fair complexion. It shouldn't have affected yours, though, with your Circassian blood.

CAPTAIN I have no Circassian blood.

GENERAL I thought you told me that you had.

CAPTAIN It was you who told me that I had.

GENERAL Some time ago, I imagine.

CAPTAIN I don't think you'll get Lawrence to recant by torture.

GENERAL Who said anything about torture? Persuasion was the word I used.

CAPTAIN (*Incredulously*) You'd argue him into it?

GENERAL Isn't that the best way of getting someone to admit he's wrong? After all, he is wrong. The Arabs' readiness for statehood is a lie and he knows it. That should give his interrogator a considerable advantage. To get him to admit that it's a lie? Difficult. With a man of faith, a real fanatic—like Feisal—impossible. But with an intellectual Englishman who believes only in his own will—and his own destiny—well, such faiths might be shaken. And another faith too—even more vulnerable—what I hear he calls his bodily integrity. One would probably have to start by teaching him a few of the facts of life.

CAPTAIN Surely if he's an intellectual he must know the facts of life. (*The* GENERAL *laughs*) Have I said something stupid?

GENERAL Don't let it concern you. (*He finishes his glass*) Yes, it's a strange relationship I have with Lawrence. He doesn't even know of my existence, while I probably already know more about him than he knows about him-

John Williams and John Mills, as GENERAL ALLENBY and LAWRENCE

self. I wish all relationships were so pleasant and uncomplicated. (*He looks at the* CAPTAIN, *who turns away*) There's one thing I don't know about him. I wonder if he really believes that all the sacrifice is worth it.
(*The* GENERAL *has poured himself another glass of wine*)

CAPTAIN Sacrifice? Sacrifice of what?

GENERAL (*Taking a sip of his wine and ruffling the* CAPTAIN'S *hair*) Oh, of everything that makes life worth living. (*The lights fade*)

SCENE THREE

Scene: A railway embankment. Reclining against a telegraph pole is LAWRENCE, *dressed in inconspicuously ragged Arab clothes. As the lights come on he is working on a pencil sketch of the railway.* HAMED *comes on, and drops down beside him. There is a silence as* LAWRENCE *continues to sketch.* HAMED *feels in his clothes for a chicken bone, which he proceeds to gnaw.*

HAMED (*At length*) Bad news.

LAWRENCE Your face told me.

HAMED They refused the money, and promised nothing.

LAWRENCE (*Still sketching*) Why?

HAMED (*Between bites*) Frightened. With good cause. Of the three men you visited in this town last month, two have been arrested and the other is in hiding. But they have his family and the families of the other two.

LAWRENCE (*After a pause*) Who talked?

HAMED One of Dakhil's children. It seems you gave him a present—an English half-penny. He showed it in the

market and tried to sell it. The great el Aurans had given it to him, he said. A policeman heard him.
(*A pause*)

LAWRENCE Is Dakhil arrested?

HAMED Yes, and Ali. It was Suleiman who escaped.

LAWRENCE (*Still sketching*) But they have his family?

HAMED Yes. Even the old grandmother. Or so they say.
(*A pause*)

LAWRENCE An English half-penny. It was there with the gold. I don't know why. Because it was bigger and brighter the child wanted it and I let him play with it. I meant to get it back from him when I left—but—I forgot. (*With sudden tension in his voice*) I forgot. (*He resumes his sketching. In a level voice*) Have they killed Dakhil and Ali?

HAMED (*Shrugging*) Let us hope so.

LAWRENCE Yes.

HAMED What are you doing?

LAWRENCE Drawing a plan of the Deraa airfield. Also that road, down there in the valley, along which our men will march—when the day comes.

HAMED Will the day come?

LAWRENCE (*Gently*) You only ask that to anger me, Hamed. It pleases you sometimes to anger me. You know the day will come.

HAMED But when?

LAWRENCE (*After a pause*) In Allah and Allenby's good time.

HAMED (*Stretching himself out*) Sometimes I think both have deserted us.

LAWRENCE They haven't—but if you talk like that, they may. And so may I.

HAMED (*Laughing*) You? (*The thought is plainly only laughable to* HAMED. *He stretches himself out, and belches happily*) What will happen after we win the war? Will you make Prince Feisal King of all Arabia?

LAWRENCE It won't be for me to make anybody king of anything, Hamed. Prince Feisal will choose for himself. Who am I to make kings?

HAMED (*After a pause*) There was a story in our camp at Azrak last night that the English King and the French President have made an agreement after the war to divide Arabia between them. The English will take all the lands beyond the Jordan and the French will take Syria and the North.
(*A pause*)

LAWRENCE (*With bland unconcern*) You have a fine ear for a story, Hamed.

HAMED The Headman of Russia—a great and noble rebel —whose name I don't remember—

LAWRENCE Lenin.

HAMED Yes, Lenin. He has told it to the world. It was an agreement made two years ago—before you came to us, el Aurans—

LAWRENCE (*Interrupting*) The great and noble rebel lies in his teeth. There is no such agreement. Could there be, and I not know?

HAMED (*After a pause*) You could be lying to us. You could have lied to us from the beginning. (*He has said it for fun, hoping to get an irritated response from* LAWRENCE. LAWRENCE, *however, does not answer nor meet his glance. Rather pathetically, after a pause*) That was a joke, el Aurans.

LAWRENCE Yes, Hamed, I know. (*He continues his sketch*) Whenever you hear this story again, will you remember that you are my friend, and beat the man who tells it?

HAMED Yes. (*Without moving*) There is a Turkish soldier walking towards us.

LAWRENCE (*Also not moving*) Did he see me sketching?

HAMED I don't know.

LAWRENCE Have you anything on you, if you are searched?

HAMED The gold and the list.

LAWRENCE Be asleep. We don't know each other. Whatever happens, have nothing to do with me.

(HAMED *obediently closes his eyes.* LAWRENCE *placidly continues to sketch as a* TURKISH SERGEANT *comes on. He walks past the two men, apparently not noticing them. Then he stops and walks back to* LAWRENCE)

SERGEANT An artist?

LAWRENCE I get pleasure in this, but I am no artist.

SERGEANT Let me see.

LAWRENCE I would not affront your Excellency's eyes.

(*He drops the sketch onto his lap*)

SERGEANT You have a white skin for these parts. What is your race?

LAWRENCE Circassian.

SERGEANT Circassian? They are rare here.

LAWRENCE Yes. We are rare.

SERGEANT What are you doing in Deraa?

LAWRENCE My business is lawful.

SERGEANT What is it?

LAWRENCE Traveling.

SERGEANT (*Looking at* HAMED) Alone?

LAWRENCE Alone.

SERGEANT Where to?

LAWRENCE Damascus.

SERGEANT On your feet, Circassian. (LAWRENCE *gets up quietly, apparently not alarmed*) You're lying, aren't you?

LAWRENCE Why should I lie to your Excellency?

SERGEANT I think you're a deserter.

LAWRENCE With respect, we Circassians are exempt from military service—

SERGEANT Don't argue. You're of military age, and therefore a deserter.

LAWRENCE The argument has force, but hardly logic. By a special decree—

SERGEANT (*Smiling*) You want logic, do you? (*He draws his revolver*) Well, here it is. (*Quite mildly*) Now come with me.

LAWRENCE Where to?

SERGEANT Why should I tell you?

(He digs him in the ribs with his revolver. LAWRENCE *drops the sketch, then stoops to pick it up. He glances at it. Then carelessly crumples it up and throws it away. It lands close to* HAMED*)*

LAWRENCE *(Going)* Why indeed, your Excellency?

(He goes off with the SERGEANT. HAMED, *as if in sleep, puts an arm out and picks up the drawing. The lights fade)*

Scene four

Scene: The lights come on slowly to reveal the TURKISH GENERAL *sitting in his room in an attitude and with an expression that denotes considerable nervous tension. He seems too to be straining to hear something, but it is not apparent what; although, at one moment, we hear a shout of harsh laughter, cut off abruptly by the evident closing of a door. After a pause the* CAPTAIN *comes in. The* GENERAL *does not look at him. The* CAPTAIN *sits in his favorite chair, and picks up a magazine.*

CAPTAIN What in the name of God is going on in the guard room?
(*There is a pause*)

GENERAL They're beating a deserter.

CAPTAIN Your orders?

GENERAL Yes.

CAPTAIN Why?

GENERAL (*After a pause*) He was insolent.

CAPTAIN I didn't see much. I don't like those sights. But I did see a white skin. At least it *was* white, I suppose?

GENERAL Yes.

CAPTAIN A Circassian?

GENERAL Yes.

CAPTAIN Do I guess accurately at the form his insolence took?

GENERAL I expect so.
(A pause)

CAPTAIN If it's reported there could be trouble.

GENERAL I don't think so.

CAPTAIN You should stop it.

GENERAL Why?

CAPTAIN They look as if they might kill him.

GENERAL He can stop it himself. He can stop it at any second. He has only to say yes.
(A pause)

CAPTAIN By the look I caught of him he's not paying you much of a compliment.

GENERAL No.
(The CAPTAIN, *after staring at the* GENERAL, *gets up suddenly)*

CAPTAIN I'm going to stop it.

GENERAL No.

CAPTAIN I'm going to. For your sake, as much as his.
(He goes to the door. The GENERAL *bars his way)*

GENERAL *(Quietly)* Now, listen carefully. It will be better for you if you don't go down there.
(The CAPTAIN, *after staring at him, walks past him and out. The* GENERAL *turns back into the room, and pours himself a glass of wine. He is pouring himself another when the* CAPTAIN *comes back, and stares at him with unbelieving eyes)*

CAPTAIN *(Violently)* Do you know who it is? *(He reads his answer in the* GENERAL'*s face)* So that's why you tried to stop me from going down there—

GENERAL I told you it would be better for you if you didn't.

CAPTAIN Is that a threat?

GENERAL Yes. Did you say anything to the men?

CAPTAIN No.

GENERAL *(Strength returning to his voice)* You will say nothing to anyone, now or at any time. If you do, I'll have you shot. He's a Circassian deserter, called Mohammed Ibn Dheilan. He comes from Kuneitra. He is being punished for insolence.

CAPTAIN (*With disgust*) Punished? Do you know what they're doing to him now?

GENERAL They've stopped beating him?

CAPTAIN Yes.

GENERAL I see.

CAPTAIN (*Hysterically*) What they're doing to him now —are those your orders too? (*There is no reply from the* GENERAL) I thought you couldn't have known—not even you, I thought, could have ordered that—

GENERAL You misjudged me.

CAPTAIN I hate the man, but this is vile and horrible.

GENERAL It's vile and horrible to be mangled in a wrecked troop train.

CAPTAIN So it's revenge—

GENERAL No. If it were I might enjoy it.

CAPTAIN What about your talk that you'd persuade him to admit he's been wrong?

GENERAL What about it?

CAPTAIN Is rape what you meant?

GENERAL I said, if you remember, that his interrogator might have to start by teaching him a few of the facts of life.

CAPTAIN (*Sitting suddenly*) And this is only the beginning?

GENERAL It may be the ending too.

CAPTAIN (*Muttering*) You mean he may die under it?

GENERAL No. They have my orders not to kill him. I mean that if my plan succeeds tonight it will be the end for him. Bodily integrity violated, will broken, enemy destroyed. (*Sharply*) There's someone on the stairs.

CAPTAIN (*At the door*) They're bringing him up. (*Hysterically*) I don't want to see it.

GENERAL Control yourself. (*The* TURKISH SERGEANT *and a* SENTRY *appear on the threshold. They are supporting* LAWRENCE *between them. He is half-conscious and his head has fallen onto his chest. Quietly*) Very well, Captain. Report to me in the morning. (*The* CAPTAIN *comes automatically to attention. Then he goes out, averting his eyes from the sight of* LAWRENCE *as he passes him. To* SERGEANT) Well? (*The* SERGEANT, *with a broad grin, nods slowly*) He said yes?
(*The* SERGEANT *shakes his head, still grinning. The* GENERAL *looks at him questioningly*)

SERGEANT (*At length*) He didn't need to say it. (*The*

GENERAL, *after a pause, nods quietly*) He's a strange one, this, General, I'm telling you.

GENERAL (*Sharply*) All right. Let him go. (*The two men release* LAWRENCE *whose knees buckle under him. He slips face downwards and motionless on to the floor*) Get out. (*The two men go. The* GENERAL *goes slowly over to* LAWRENCE. *He kneels down and, quite gently, pulls his head back and looks at him. Quietly*) You must understand that I know. (*He replaces* LAWRENCE'S *head gently on the floor*) You can hear me, I think. (*Slowly repeating*) You must understand that I know. (*There is no sign from* LAWRENCE *that he has heard. Throughout the ensuing scene he remains completely motionless. The* GENERAL *pours a glass of wine and takes it over to* LAWRENCE. *He thrusts it in front of his face, but* LAWRENCE *makes no movement. The* GENERAL *puts the glass on the floor beside* LAWRENCE *and then stands near him, looking down*) I do pity you, you know. You won't ever believe it, but it's true. I know what was revealed to you tonight, and I know what that revelation will have done to you. You can think I mean just a broken will, if you like. That might have destroyed you by itself. But I mean more than that. Far more. (*Angrily*) But why did you leave yourself so vulnerable? What's the use of learning if it doesn't teach you to know yourself as you really are? (*Pause*) It's a pity your desert adventure couldn't have ended cleanly, in front of a firing squad. But that's for lesser enemies—not for you. (*He kneels down*) For you, killing wasn't enough. (*He lifts* LAWRENCE'S *head again*) You had to be—destroyed. (*He lowers* LAWRENCE'S *head, and stands up*) The door at the bottom of the stairs through there is unlocked. It leads into the street.

(He walks into his bedroom. LAWRENCE, *at length, waveringly thrusts out a hand towards the glass of wine. He draws it to him and drains it. Then, painfully and slowly, he begins to drag himself across the floor towards the other door. The lights fade)*

Scene five

Scene: Before the lights come on we hear the sound of a military band playing a jaunty march, and the sound of voices and laughter.

PHOTOGRAPHER'S VOICE (*From darkness*) Hold it, General. (*There is a flash from the darkness, and the sound of general laughter. The lights go on to show a room in* ALLENBY'S *field headquarters.* ALLENBY, STORRS, BARRINGTON, *the* A.D.C., FRANKS, *now a war correspondent, and a* PHOTOGRAPHER *are all present. Everyone seems very jovial. A band is playing outside. It is* ALLENBY *who has just had his photograph taken*)

FRANKS I think, if you don't mind, General, just one more. And this time can we, perhaps, have a slightly more triumphant expression.

ALLENBY What? More triumphant? I thought I'd made myself odiously so in that one.

FRANKS Forgive me, sir, but you really didn't look as if you'd just won a great battle.

ALLENBY How does one look as if one had just won a great battle? What do you suggest, Storrs?

STORRS A rather bored and impassive expression, sir, as if taking Jerusalem was something that happened to you every day.

FRANKS No, no. Not bored. Impassive, if you like, but stern and unyielding and—well—victorious. Now shall we try again, sir? (*To* PHOTOGRAPHER) Ready? (*The* PHOTOGRAPHER *nods*) Right, sir, if you don't mind. (ALLENBY *does as bidden*) Just a little to the left. That's right. Now—can we try that expression?

ALLENBY (*Muttering*) Oh God, this is agony.

FRANKS It won't last very long, sir. (ALLENBY *tries an unyielding expression*) No. That isn't quite right.

STORRS Of course a backcloth of Jerusalem would help. And what about some Turkish prisoners, lying on the floor in chains.

ALLENBY Careful, Storrs. That appointment isn't official yet.

FRANKS What appointment is that?

ALLENBY Military Governor of Jerusalem.

FRANKS Oh. Good. (*To* STORRS) We must take a photograph of you.

STORRS (*Cowering*) Oh no.

ALLENBY (*Laughing*) Oh yes. And get him to look gubernatorial.

FRANKS (*Patiently*) Now, sir. Can we try again? (ALLENBY *poses*) Now think of Jerusalem.

ALLENBY (*Through his teeth*) Jerusalem I've got. I'm thinking of Damascus.

BARRINGTON (*Admiring his expression*) Very good, sir. That has the real Wellington look.

ALLENBY Quiet, Brigadier—unless you want to be a Colonel again.

BARRINGTON (*Aggrieved*) I meant it seriously, sir.

FRANKS Hold it, General. (*The flashlight is released again and the photograph taken.* ALLENBY *relaxes with relief*) Perhaps just one more—

ALLENBY No, certainly not. (*Pointing to a tray of drinks*) Have a drink, gentlemen, and then leave me to fight my war.

(BARRINGTON, STORRS, *and the* A.D.C. *go towards the tray, where the* A.D.C. *pours them drinks. The* PHOTOGRAPHER *begins to pack up his apparatus*)

FRANKS (*To* ALLENBY, *with notebook now handy*) There's not very much more of your war left to fight, is there, General?

ALLENBY (*Sharply*) There certainly is, and please don't give people at home any other impression. The Turkish Army is by no means beaten. It's suffered a defeat, but it's retiring in good order. There are many more battles to come and they'll become increasingly harder as the Turks shorten their lines of communication.

PHOTOGRAPHER (*At door*) Will that be all, Mr. Franks?

FRANKS Yes. Thank you. (*As* PHOTOGRAPHER *prepares to leave*) Just a moment. (*To* ALLENBY) We've rigged up a makeshift studio next door. Is there any hope of enticing you there tomorrow?

ALLENBY I'm afraid I'm far too busy.

FRANKS Pity. (*To* PHOTOGRAPHER) All right.

PHOTOGRAPHER Goodnight, gentlemen.
(*He goes*)

FRANKS I've just one last request, sir.

ALLENBY Come and have a whisky and soda while you make it.
(*They join* BARRINGTON *and* STORRS)

FRANKS My editor is very anxious for me to get an interview with Major Lawrence.

ALLENBY I've no doubt he is.

FRANKS Could I have your authority?

ALLENBY My authority over Lawrence is sketchy, at the best of times. As regards an interview—even with you—I should say it was non-existent. Do you agree, Storrs?

STORRS I would imagine that it might be rather easier for Mr. Franks to get an interview with the Dalai Lama—

ALLENBY Besides, when last heard from he was at Deraa, some hundred and fifty miles behind the enemy lines—

BARRINGTON No, sir. He's here. Didn't you know?

ALLENBY (*Bewildered*) Here?

BARRINGTON Yes, sir. I saw him an hour ago. He was waiting to see you, he said. I'm sorry, sir, I thought you must have been told.

ALLENBY (*To* A.D.C.) Did you know?

A.D.C. No, sir.

ALLENBY Well, go and get him at once.

A.D.C. Yes, sir.
(*He goes out*)

ALLENBY Lawrence waiting? Usually he doesn't even knock. I look up and he's standing facing me. (*To* STORRS) I'd have thought he'd have let you know, at least.

STORRS (*Shrugging*) I've ceased to speculate. It's unfruitful.

ALLENBY Anyway he's here, which is the main thing, and he couldn't have come at a better time. I suppose he knew exactly when I'd take Jerusalem, although, God knows I didn't. The man's prescience is satanic.

FRANKS May I stay, sir, for a moment?

ALLENBY Yes, if you like. I doubt if it'll be much use to you. Storrs, get me a whisky and soda—

A.D.C. (*Opening the door*) Major Lawrence.
(LAWRENCE *comes in, walking with a limp that he is evidently at pains to conceal. He is in Arab clothes*)

ALLENBY Why didn't you let me know you were here?

LAWRENCE I understood you were busy with the press.

ALLENBY (*With a glance at* FRANKS) Ah. I see. This gentleman is the culprit. Mr. Franks, Major Lawrence.

LAWRENCE (*Politely*) How do you do.

ALLENBY (*Taking his whisky from* STORRS) Oh, thank you.

STORRS Hullo, T.E.

LAWRENCE Hullo.

BARRINGTON Hullo, Lawrence. Have you hurt yourself? You're limping a bit.

LAWRENCE An accident with a camel. I got dragged through some barbed wire.

ALLENBY (*Mischievously*) I think Mr. Franks has a request to make of you, Lawrence.

LAWRENCE (*Turning politely to* FRANKS) Oh really?

FRANKS (*Nervously*) Well—Major—we war correspondents have our duty to perform like everyone else—so don't be too harsh with me. But you realize that the public interest about you at home has become pretty intense lately and colorful figures are rare enough in this war, and—(*Glancing nervously at* ALLENBY *and* STORRS, *who are plainly enjoying their anticipation of* LAWRENCE'S *response*) Well, I suppose I'd just better come straight out with it. Can I have an interview?

LAWRENCE When?

FRANKS Well—tomorrow.

LAWRENCE What time?

FRANKS Any time that would suit you. Ten o'clock?

LAWRENCE Yes. Where?

FRANKS Well, anywhere, but of course, what would be far

the best would be if you would come along to the studio I've rigged up—and then we could get some really beautiful photographs.

LAWRENCE Where is your studio?

FRANKS (*Hardly able to believe his luck*) Next door to here.

ALLENBY (*Approaching* LAWRENCE *with a slightly worried frown*) He has backcloths at his studio.

FRANKS (*Writing feverishly*) Oh, General, you go on far too much about those backcloths. A photographic cloth can be quite plain, you know. Would you allow yourself to be photographed in front of a backcloth?

LAWRENCE Whatever you think best.

FRANKS Good. Oh, good. Ten o'clock, then? (LAWRENCE *nods*) You're not going to let me down, are you?

LAWRENCE No, I'll see you tomorrow.

FRANKS Thank you, Major. (*To* ALLENBY) Goodnight, sir. (*To the others*) Goodnight.

(*He goes.* STORRS, *conscious of an atmosphere, hastily finishes his whisky*)

STORRS We'd better leave you too, sir.

ALLENBY (*Looking at* LAWRENCE) If you would.

STORRS (*Casually to* LAWRENCE) I hope I shall see something of you while you're here.

LAWRENCE I won't be here long.

STORRS (*To* ALLENBY) Well, goodbye, sir.
(*He goes*)

BARRINGTON Could I have just two words with Lawrence, sir? Rather important. (ALLENBY *nods.* BARRINGTON *turns to* LAWRENCE) I've had a rather sharp inquiry from the Foreign Office regarding the question of so-called atrocities on your front—

LAWRENCE I have no front.

BARRINGTON Well, during your raids and ambushes and things. It's been alleged through a neutral embassy that you don't take prisoners. (*He awaits a response from* LAWRENCE. *He remains silent*) An official denial from you would help enormously.

LAWRENCE (*Politely*) Then you shall have it.

BARRINGTON Good. Would you let me have it tomorrow, in writing?

LAWRENCE In writing? (BARRINGTON *nods*) All right.

BARRINGTON Thank you.
(*He turns to go*)

LAWRENCE The Arabs have been less demanding. My denials to them on more important issues are confined to the verbal.

BARRINGTON (*Stopping short*) You mean the denial would be untrue?

LAWRENCE Not entirely untrue. Misleading is a better word. We do take prisoners—when we are not being chased, and can spare the men to escort them to Feisal and I've managed to keep some control of the situation. A combination of those contingencies is unhappily rare.

BARRINGTON But this admission is very serious.

LAWRENCE (*Raising his voice slightly*) I agree. Did the neutral embassy have anything to say about the Turkish treatment of Arab prisoners?

BARRINGTON No, but if there have been reprisals—

LAWRENCE (*With a sharp laugh*) Reprisals? The old game of who started it? Who's to say? And does it matter? I can only tell you that for a long time now no wounded Arab soldier has been left on the field for the Turks to take. If we can't move him we shoot him.

BARRINGTON (*Hotly*) Listen, Lawrence—the Turk's a clean fighter.

LAWRENCE I've no doubt, General, but ours isn't a clean war. It's an Asiatic revolution, and a European who tries to direct the course of such a thing is apt to find himself rather out of his depth.

BARRINGTON But–

ALLENBY (*Interposing*) That's enough, Barrington. You can see Lawrence tomorrow.

BARRINGTON Yes, sir.
(*He salutes punctiliously, turns on his heels and goes*)

ALLENBY Don't worry about that.

LAWRENCE No, sir. I won't.

ALLENBY You made it sound pretty grim, I must say.

LAWRENCE I could have made it sound grimmer.

ALLENBY Well, you've come at a good time.

LAWRENCE Yes, sir. Congratulations.

ALLENBY Thank you. Tell me, how did you get the news?

LAWRENCE I didn't, until I reached here.

ALLENBY What did you come for, then?

LAWRENCE To ask you to find me another job.
(*A pause*)

ALLENBY What other job?

LAWRENCE Any one at all, providing that it has nothing whatever to do with the Arab Revolt. At a pinch I suppose I could still draw you some quite useful maps.

ALLENBY (*Nodding, at length*) I see. Go on.

LAWRENCE Is my request granted?

ALLENBY It may be. Go on. Tell me why you wish to relinquish your present post.

LAWRENCE You're going to make it hard for me, are you?

ALLENBY (*Quietly*) I see no reason to make it easy.

LAWRENCE Yes. I admire you for that. You want my excuses for desertion?

ALLENBY Your reasons.

LAWRENCE (*Nodding appreciatively*) Very well. (*Quietly matter of fact*) I have come to believe that the Arab Revolt is a fake, founded on deceit and sustained by lies, and I want no further part in it.

ALLENBY (*Making notes*) Go on.

LAWRENCE On the military side I have only failure to report. The bridge at Yarmuk has not been blown and Arab forces have at no time successfully intervened in your campaign to date.

ALLENBY (*Quietly, continuing writing*) Yes?

LAWRENCE To sum up, the whole venture is morally, militarily and financially unjustifiable—a total washout, and should be abandoned. (*After a pause*) Anyway, I can't go on. (*He looks at* ALLENBY, *who makes an impassive final note, laying down his pen*) However, if you don't agree with what I've said about the Arab Revolt and want me to suggest someone to take my place—

ALLENBY (*Quietly*) There is no one to take your place. Now, dealing with your points in reverse order and leaving out the last. (*Looking at his notes*) Your military failure is untrue, even after taking into account your tendency for histrionic exaggeration. I haven't required Arab intervention yet in my campaign, and I don't expect you to succeed in blowing up every damn bridge I ask you to destroy. The Arab Revolt a fake? That's for you to say, but you told me once that you could will yourself into believing it wasn't.

LAWRENCE I think it was you who told me. Anyway, my will has proved less trustworthy than I thought.

ALLENBY What's happened, Lawrence?

LAWRENCE (*Suddenly tired*) Can't we say battle weariness?

ALLENBY No. Not for you.

LAWRENCE Disillusionment, cowardice—?

ALLENBY No. Something extraordinary happened. What?

LAWRENCE I had a vision. It happens to people in the desert.

ALLENBY A vision of what?

LAWRENCE Of the truth.

ALLENBY About the Arab Revolt?

LAWRENCE No. About myself.

ALLENBY And the truth is (*Tapping his notes*) "I can't go on"?

LAWRENCE That's part of the truth.

ALLENBY The most important part, isn't it?

LAWRENCE No. Only the most relevant.
(*A pause*)

ALLENBY (*Suddenly*) What a pity! What an awful pity. (LAWRENCE *looks at the floor saying nothing.* ALLENBY *gets up brusquely*) All right. I'll send you back to England.

LAWRENCE I haven't asked for that.

ALLENBY The War Office should be glad to have you. You're due for promotion, so I'll appoint you Lieutenant

Colonel. I've also recommended you—some weeks ago—for the D.S.O. so with that and your C.B. and your wound stripes you should make quite a show there. (*The* SENTRY *appears*) Yes?

SENTRY Mr. Storrs has an urgent telegram.

ALLENBY Send him in.

SENTRY Yes, sir.
(LAWRENCE *gets up to go*)

ALLENBY No, stay. I want a word with you about your successor.
(STORRS *comes in*)

STORRS (*Handing* ALLENBY *a telegram*) Downing Street, sir. They want you to make a triumphal entry into Jerusalem on Wednesday.

ALLENBY What do they think I am? A Roman Emperor?

STORRS Brass bands, victory marches, beautiful girls hurling flowers at us. I'm looking forward to it. (*To* LAWRENCE) Your man Hamed is outside. Wants to see you.

LAWRENCE He should have gone. I ordered him back to Prince Feisal's camp two hours ago.

STORRS Well, he's determined to talk to you. Seems very agitated. When are you going back, T.E.?

ALLENBY *(With sudden harshness)* He's not going back.

STORRS What?

ALLENBY He feels he can't go on any more. He's had all that flesh and blood will stand. I see his point. I'm sending him to the War Office.

LAWRENCE *(Looking at the ground)* May I go, sir? I'm feeling tired. We can talk about my—successor some other time.

ALLENBY *(Carelessly)* Very well. *(As* LAWRENCE *reaches the door)* Just one moment. I shall want you to take part in this entry on Wednesday.

LAWRENCE In what capacity?

ALLENBY Chief British Liaison Officer to Arab Forces in the field, of course.

LAWRENCE *(Murmuring)* No, sir.

ALLENBY *(Coldly)* It's an order. You will march directly behind me, and attend all the various ceremonies at my side.

LAWRENCE *(With a sudden hard laugh)* Oh yes. Good text-book stuff. *(Indicating the telegram)* A General should be ready at one instant to exploit any opportunity suddenly laid open to him—

ALLENBY (*Coldly*) You seem to think my order is a punishment. It isn't. The honor that is being done to you on Wednesday is an award for your past. If it gives you uncomfortable thoughts about your present that's your affair, and not mine.

LAWRENCE (*Now suddenly weary*) And that's from the same textbook, isn't it? How to deal with deserters. I've learnt how to deal with them too—but not from Sandhurst training. From experience. Sad, scared, broken-willed little creatures—you can't persuade them or threaten them or even joke them back into battle. But sometimes you can shame them back. It's surprising how often—if you use the right technique. (*In a voice drained of emotion*) You know, I think that I admire you more than any man on earth, and I've never admired you more than I do at this moment. On my way here I had worked out for myself every stratagem you might use to get me to go back, and had planned all my moves to counter them. But, I'm beaten in five minutes. Can I see my bodyguard? Storrs says he's outside.

ALLENBY (*Calling*) Sentry!

SENTRY (*Appearing*) Sir?

ALLENBY Get Major Lawrence's Arab servant.

SENTRY Yes, sir.
(*He goes out*)

LAWRENCE I suppose what I left out of account is the

splendid core of cruelty that all great Generals should have. (HAMED *comes in*) Hamed, why are you still in Gaza? You had my strict orders to return to Prince Feisal's Camp. Is that not so?

HAMED (*Murmuring*) It is so, el Aurans.

LAWRENCE Why then have you disobeyed me?

HAMED My camel has died.

LAWRENCE (*Gently*) Has it? She seemed all right this morning.

HAMED A sudden illness must have struck her, el Aurans.

LAWRENCE Yes. Very sudden. There was my camel—

HAMED (*Looking at the ground*) She has died too.

LAWRENCE Of the same illness?

HAMED Assuredly. (*Looking up at* LAWRENCE) So now I must stay with you, here, el Aurans. There is now no means of leaving, is there?

LAWRENCE Until you find another camel.

HAMED In Gaza they are hard to find.

LAWRENCE By Thursday morning, you must have found two new camels—

HAMED *Two–?*

LAWRENCE (*Continuing*) Two fine, fast camels every bit as good as those you have just got rid of.

HAMED (*His face lighting up with joy*) In an hour–

LAWRENCE Listen. Thursday at the first light of dawn. (*With a look at* ALLENBY) I have a duty to perform in Jerusalem on Wednesday.

HAMED This is not a joke?

LAWRENCE No.

HAMED But you said–

LAWRENCE You should not always confuse what I say with what I do. (HAMED *bows suddenly to* LAWRENCE, *takes his hand, kisses it, and then places it on his head, Arab fashion. Then he turns and goes out quickly.* LAWRENCE *shrugs his shoulders, facing* ALLENBY) Well, sir, I told you my will isn't what it was.

ALLENBY I think it'll mend.

LAWRENCE No. I'll have to try and find a substitute. (*Turning away*) But there are just two things I wish you knew.

ALLENBY What?

LAWRENCE The kind of deserter you're sending back. And the kind of battle you're sending him back to—
(LAWRENCE *goes. There is a pause*)

STORRS You'd have made as good a diplomat as a soldier.

ALLENBY I deserve the insult.

STORRS No insult. But were you right to get him to go back?

ALLENBY (*Angrily*) Am I supposed to care about what's right? It was necessary. That's all that concerns me. (*Unhappily*) All that ought to concern me. (*He gets up and goes to pour himself a drink. With a sigh*) Oh God, Storrs, won't it be wonderful when this damned war's over.
(*The lights fade*)

Scene six

In the darkness we hear the distant rumble of heavy gunfire.

Scene: Outside LAWRENCE'S *tent.* LAWRENCE *himself is shaving, using a canvas basin and a mirror hung up on a pole. A young R.A.F. officer* (HIGGINS) *comes out of the tent with some typescript in his hand. The gunfire continues throughout the scene.*

HIGGINS I've done it, sir. I hope I've got it all right. Would you check it as soon as possible?

LAWRENCE Does your pilot want to take off?

HIGGINS Well—it's getting a bit late, sir, and the C-in-C is waiting for this. Highest priority.

LAWRENCE Read it to me.

HIGGINS (*Reading*) "Operations of 25th and 26th September, 1918. I decided to place the main Arab force in the direct path of the Turkish Fourth Army's line of retreat. My staff considered this a hazardous enterprise, in view of the fact that the Fourth Army was retreating intact to cover Damascus. They thought that our untried force, outnumbered by roughly four to one, might prove no match for disciplined troops. I, on the other hand, reckoned that the element of surprise would outweigh this disadvantage.

I am glad to report that events have justified my unweary optimism."

LAWRENCE Unweary? This report has enough hubris in it without your adding to it. I said unwary.

HIGGINS (*Brightly*) Oh. Sorry, sir. Unwary. (*He makes a correction*) And what was the other word you used? Hu— something?

LAWRENCE Hubris. It's the Greek for showing-off.

HIGGINS Oh but, sir—I mean—surely you've got something (*Indicating report*) to show off about, I'd say.

LAWRENCE You think so?

HIGGINS The Turks caught in a trap between our chaps in the south and your chaps up here. I mean it's bloody marvelous, sir. (*There is no reply*) Bloody marvelous. (*Continuing to read*) "I am happy to report that the Fourth Turkish Army has, since eleven hundred hours this morning, ceased to exist. A detailed report of the operation follows—"

LAWRENCE (*Interrupting*) Very well. As I have your sanction for hubris, you might as well add this to the main report. After "ceased to exist"— (HIGGINS *has his pencil and pad*) In view of this situation it is my intention to enter the City of Damascus at first light tomorrow, and to hold it in the name and authority of Prince Feisal. I assume this action will meet with your approval—an assumption forced on me by the fact that should it not it will anyway be too late for you to inform me.

HIGGINS My gosh I'll be able to write my memoirs after the war. *Lawrence of Arabia and I* by S. R. Higgins.

LAWRENCE (*Interrupting*) Did you invent that name?

HIGGINS What? Higgins?

LAWRENCE No. The other one.

HIGGINS Lawrence of Arabia? Good heavens, no, sir. That's what the press have been calling you for months.

LAWRENCE Have they? I didn't know.
(*He sits down on the ground, Arab fashion, his face expressionless but lost in thought*)

HIGGINS Shall I read the detailed stuff, sir?

LAWRENCE No. You'd better take off. Was there anything that seemed wrong to you in it?

HIGGINS (*Doubtfully*) No. Well—there was just one thing—
(*He stops, looking rather scared*)

LAWRENCE What's that?

HIGGINS The night raid on that station.

LAWRENCE What about it?

HIGGINS There's something in it, I wonder if it's wise to— I mean it is an official report.

LAWRENCE Read it.

HIGGINS (*Reading*) "Operations of September 18th." (*Murmuring*) "In order to complete the encirclement of Deraa —a night assault on the railway—surprise not wholly achieved—" ah. Here we are, sir. "Ordering the Zaali to give covering fire I went down the embankment with my personal bodyguard and laid charges. These were successfully detonated, and the bridge destroyed, but the enemy now directed his fire at the bridge, my companion being badly hit at the first burst. I attempted to drag him up the embankment but without success and, as the Turks were beginning to issue from their blockhouse, I had no recourse but to leave him, after carrying out the usual practice in such cases. I rejoined the troop, and the retirement was completed without further loss."

(*He stops.* LAWRENCE *is still looking at the ground*)

LAWRENCE (*At length*) What part specifically do you object to?

HIGGINS Well, sir, the implication.

LAWRENCE That I killed the man that was wounded?

HIGGINS Yes, sir.

LAWRENCE But I did kill him.

HIGGINS (*Shocked*) Oh. Well– (*Defiantly*) But it's not the kind of thing you say in an official report.

LAWRENCE Isn't it? I describe later on how we killed four thousand Turks.

HIGGINS (*Horrified*) Yes–but they're the enemy and this is one of your own men.

LAWRENCE Yes.

HIGGINS Of course, I know he was only an Arab, but still it does sound–do forgive me, sir–a bit–callous.

LAWRENCE I see. And you'd like me to make it sound less callous?

HIGGINS I really think you should take it out altogether, sir. I mean, there might be trouble with his wife or something–

LAWRENCE He didn't have a wife. He once had a friend, but he's dead too.

HIGGINS (*A little cross at* LAWRENCE'S *lack of imagination*) Well, I'm sure he must have had someone who'll care about his death–

LAWRENCE Yes, he did. But I doubt if that person will give much trouble.

HIGGINS Well, you never know. Anyway, sir—have I your permission to edit the passage a little? I could just say the burst of machine-gun fire missed you but killed him instantly.

LAWRENCE (*Politely*) A very happy invention.

HIGGINS I'll do it when I get to H.Q. Goodbye, sir.

LAWRENCE (*Getting up*) Goodbye.
(AUDA ABU TAYI *strides on. He looks angry, hot and weary. His clothes are torn and bloodstained*)

AUDA Who would have thought the day would come when Auda would grow tired of killing Turks? (*He throws down his rifle*) Old age is a terrible thing.

HIGGINS (*To* LAWRENCE) Well, sir, I'll be off.

AUDA (*Squinting at him venomously*) By Allah—a Turk. (*He picks up his rifle*)

LAWRENCE No. No—British.

AUDA (*Accusingly*) I know the British uniform. That is a Turk.

LAWRENCE No. An officer in King George's Air Force. (*To* HIGGINS) You'd better clear off. He thinks you're the enemy.

HIGGINS Oh Lord!—I say—what a scruffy-looking old wog, or is he one of your Generals?

LAWRENCE Yes. That's exactly what he is.

HIGGINS Gosh! Poor old Higgins. Always putting his foot in it. Well–goodbye, sir.
(He salutes again, turns and meets AUDA's *darkly suspicious gaze. Rather nervously he salutes him too, and then goes)*

AUDA *(Wearily)* Well, my friend, is it over?

LAWRENCE Yes.

AUDA Tomorrow–Damascus?

LAWRENCE Yes.

AUDA Our enemy destroyed and the dream of two years fulfilled. Damascus! Allah indeed is good.

LAWRENCE Allah is good.
(Pause. AUDA *looks at* LAWRENCE *with thoughtful and sympathetic eyes)*

AUDA They have told me about Hamed.

LAWRENCE I would not have told you.

AUDA I am the one you should have told.

LAWRENCE It's not a tale that should be told to a friend.

AUDA Who else but a friend?

LAWRENCE An enemy—or a stranger. To anyone but a friend.

AUDA (*Gently*) Let's speak of other things. Let's speak of yesterday's great battle.
(*A pause*)

LAWRENCE He opened his eyes for a moment when I lifted my revolver. He had them tightly closed until that moment. He was in great pain. But it was the will of fate that he should open his eyes and see me pointing the revolver at his head. He said "Rashid will be angry with you, el Aurans."

AUDA I remember Rashid. He died on our march in the desert.

LAWRENCE Yes. The day I failed with my compass. So then I said, "Salute Rashid from me," and he smiled. Then the pain came back and he closed his eyes again. Just as I was lifting the revolver once more to his head he said, "God will give you peace." Then I fired. The Turks were already coming out of the blockhouse.
(*A pause*)

AUDA The memory of it will not always be so sharp.

LAWRENCE I once said the same to Hamed. He didn't believe it then and nor do I now.

AUDA You must think of other things. Think of Damascus and what we must do there.

LAWRENCE Yes.

AUDA And all that we must do after Damascus. Only now does our fight truly begin. (*Anxiously*) You will go on fighting with us and for us, el Aurans? For Allah knows we will need you in peace even more than we have in war.

LAWRENCE Yes. I suppose I must try and make amends—

AUDA Amends?

LAWRENCE To the people I've misled.
(*A pause*)

AUDA By Allah, I think your victories have made you mad. Have you misled us all from Mecca to Damascus—a thousand miles and more—against an enemy many times our strength?

LAWRENCE Forgive me, Auda. It was a feeble joke.

AUDA You will fight for us in peace as you fought for us in war?

LAWRENCE Yes. To the limits of my strength. Can I say more?

AUDA No. For what limits are there to the strength of el Aurans?

LAWRENCE Some, I think.

AUDA None, I know. (*He embraces* LAWRENCE) I have lost many sons—yes, and grandsons—but for none of them did I grieve so much as I did for you—that day when you left us and went to Gaza and we thought you had gone for ever. What time tonight?

LAWRENCE Midnight. We shall be in Damascus by dawn. (BARRINGTON *comes on hurriedly*)

BARRINGTON Ah, Lawrence. Good. I'm glad I've found you. You really ought to leave clearer indications about the exact site of your headquarters. You see—
(AUDA, *under the stress of an evidently stormy emotion, clutches* BARRINGTON'S *tunic, and pulls him to him*)

AUDA Who are you?

BARRINGTON My name's Barrington. General Barrington—G.H.Q.

AUDA (*Fiercely*) Tell them, G.H.Q., tell them in England what I Auda Abu Tayi say of el Aurans. Of Manhood (*He shakes* BARRINGTON) the man. Of Freedom (*He shakes him again*) free. A spirit (*He shakes him a third time*) without equal. I see no flaw in him. And if any offal-eating traitor should ever deny the greatness of that man (*Pointing to* LAWRENCE) may the curse of Auda fall upon his dung-filled head.
(*He shakes* BARRINGTON *a fourth time, then releases him abruptly and strides out*)

BARRINGTON One of your chaps?

LAWRENCE Yes.

BARRINGTON The Bedouin are excitable people. Far too excitable.

LAWRENCE How did you get up here?

BARRINGTON By armored car from Deraa. I was with the Fourth Cavalry Division when they entered the town this morning. The G.O.C. sent me here to find you and bring you down there to him at once.

LAWRENCE Oh? Under arrest?

BARRINGTON (*Impatiently*) No, of course not, but he's raging—absolutely raging—and God knows—after the sights I saw this morning—I don't blame him. Apparently some of your wogs sneaked into the place last night—

LAWRENCE May we make our language more official, General? A contingent of Prince Feisal's Arab forces, acting under my orders, last night captured the important road and rail center of Deraa—

BARRINGTON Yes, I daresay that's how it'll go down in your report. Listen, I'm a fairly hardened soldier, Lawrence, but in all my life I've never seen anything like it. It's utterly sickening. They've been burning and looting everything Turkish they can find—massacring the garrison—there are only a handful of survivors. We've even had to surround the military hospital. It's a dangerous situation, and, as you seem to be the only person who can control these savages, you've got to come down with me now at once—

LAWRENCE (*Coldly*) I'm sorry, but I'm afraid I can't spare the time.
(*A pause*)

BARRINGTON (*Wide-eyed*) Shall I report that to the G.O.C.?

LAWRENCE You will anyway, so why ask me? You can also tell the G.O.C. that I suggest he orders his troops out of a town which was captured and is now being securely held by mine. And now—General—if you don't mind, I have an important operation planned for tonight, and I must prepare for it—
(*He turns to go.* BARRINGTON *runs to bar his way*)

BARRINGTON I'm getting pretty tired of these schoolboy jokes of yours, Lawrence.

LAWRENCE (*Amused*) Schoolboy jokes? How interesting. I've grown up a bit since we first met at Abdullah's camp. Or hadn't you noticed?

BARRINGTON Your suggestion is serious? (LAWRENCE *shrugs*) That Deraa be left in the hands of those savages?

LAWRENCE (*Quietly*) It may be that some of those savages come from a village called Tafas. We followed the Turks into it two days ago. Outside the village we saw a child with a bayonet wound in his neck—but he was still alive.

When I bent over him, he screamed "Don't hit me, Baba." Then he ran away from us until he fell over and died. That was only the first thing we saw. When we went into the village and saw the bodies of eighteen women, all bayoneted obscenely, two of them pregnant, I said "The best of you brings me the most Turkish dead." I note, General, with interest that my wishes were apparently carried out last night in Deraa. (*A thought striking him*) In Deraa? How stupid! I hadn't realized. In Deraa? (*He laughs softly. He makes a move to go.* BARRINGTON *stops him forcibly*)

BARRINGTON Are you quite lost to all human feeling? (LAWRENCE *laughs again, with now a different note*)

LAWRENCE Do you know, General, I think you're right. That's exactly what I am. (*His laugh grows louder, with a shade of hysteria in it*) Quite lost to all human feeling.

BARRINGTON (*Appalled*) I think you're a callous, soulless, sadistic little brute.

LAWRENCE (*Still laughing, eagerly*) Yes, yes, oh yes. Especially soulless.

BARRINGTON You sicken me.
(*He pushes* LAWRENCE *away violently so that he falls down, still laughing, but weakly now.* BARRINGTON *goes out*)

LAWRENCE (*Calling after him*) I sicken myself. That's the joke. Not a schoolboy joke. Just–a–joke. (*The laughter*

is no longer laughter, but the sound continues) Lawrence of Arabia—the soulless wonder—
(Suddenly a quiet, clear voice—actual not recorded—cuts through the sound that LAWRENCE *is making)*

HAMED'S VOICE God will give you peace.

LAWRENCE *(Struggling to his feet)* No, Hamed, never. Never in this life.
(He goes out unsteadily)

HAMED'S VOICE *(As* LAWRENCE *disappears)* God will give you peace.
(The lights fade)

SCENE SEVEN

Loud and clear comes a bugle call, playing the reveille. The lights come up.

Scene: The FLIGHT LIEUTENANT'S *office. He is sitting at the desk, looking up in bewilderment at an* R.A.F. CORPORAL.

FLIGHT LIEUTENANT What? But I don't understand. The Group Captain coming to see me? Are you sure?

CORPORAL On his way, sir.

FLIGHT LIEUTENANT But why didn't he tell me to come and see him?

CORPORAL Don't know, sir.

FLIGHT LIEUTENANT Well, it's very odd. Thank you. (*He begins hastily to clear up his desk, moving a few documents from the "In" tray to the "Out" tray, and emptying an overfull ashtray. There is a peremptory knock. Nervously*) Come in. (*The* GROUP CAPTAIN *comes in. He is only half dressed and looks disheveled and harassed. The* CORPORAL *springs to attention*) Why, sir. This is a surprise. I don't often have the honor—

GROUP CAPTAIN Corporal, tell the Flight Sergeant of B Flight to report to me here immediately.

CORPORAL Yes, sir.

(He goes out)

GROUP CAPTAIN *(Hoarsely)* Do you keep any drink here?

FLIGHT LIEUTENANT A little—er—medicinal, sir.

(He opens a cupboard and takes out a bottle of whisky and a glass)

GROUP CAPTAIN I need it. My office has become a nightmare. The telephone hasn't stopped since six this morning, when the duty officer woke me with the news. *(Taking the glass and drinking)* Now I'm not at all sure it isn't being tapped. Probably the *Daily Mirror*. They were the first on. Thanks. Cheers. *(He takes another swig and hands the glass back to the bewildered* FLIGHT LIEUTENANT*)* Now, listen, we've got to get this fellow off the station within an hour—

FLIGHT LIEUTENANT Which fellow?

GROUP CAPTAIN *(Impatiently)* Ross, of course. Air Ministry are most insistent that there aren't any photographs, so I suggest we smuggle him through my private gate. Agreed?

FLIGHT LIEUTENANT Er—excuse me, sir, I'm just the least little bit behind. Do I agree that we smuggle Aircraftman Ross off the station, through your own private gate? That was the question, wasn't it?

GROUP CAPTAIN Oh, my God! You don't know? No, I suppose you wouldn't. We're trying to keep it as dark as possible, though everyone will know tonight—

FLIGHT LIEUTENANT (*Patiently*) Has it anything to do with the charge I put him on for hearing by you this morning?

GROUP CAPTAIN You put him on a charge?

FLIGHT LIEUTENANT Yes, sir. Gross insubordination.

GROUP CAPTAIN Who to?

FLIGHT LIEUTENANT Me.
(*A pause*)

GROUP CAPTAIN (*Solicitously*) I think you'd better have a nip of your own whisky.

FLIGHT LIEUTENANT (*Virtuously*) Never touch it in the morning.

GROUP CAPTAIN Well, I will. (*Muttering*) A charge? God. If the *Mirror* got hold of that. (*He takes another glass from the* FLIGHT LIEUTENANT) You know who it was you've charged with insubordination? Lawrence of Arabia.

FLIGHT LIEUTENANT (*After a pause, confidently*) Oh no. Oh no. That can't be. I mean—

GROUP CAPTAIN How exactly was he insubordinate?

FLIGHT LIEUTENANT He was late on pass. I asked him who he'd been with, that night. He said the Archbishop of

Canterbury (*His voice begins to falter*) Lord and Lady Astor, and Mr. and Mrs. George Bernard—oh my God!

GROUP CAPTAIN (*Holding out the bottle*) Here.

FLIGHT LIEUTENANT (*Taking it*) But it's unbelievable. Why has he done it?

GROUP CAPTAIN Well, that's the question. It's very difficult to get anything out of him. I had an hour with him, nearly. A bit awkward. I had to ask him to sit, of course.

FLIGHT LIEUTENANT Of course.

GROUP CAPTAIN Kept on using the one word, refuge. The R.A.F. was his refuge.

FLIGHT LIEUTENANT From what?

GROUP CAPTAIN God knows. From himself and his reputation, he said. He wanted a number, not a name. Very insistent about his number. Lets him lose his identity. One of a mass. Fellow's a bit screwy, if you ask me.

FLIGHT LIEUTENANT (*Excitedly*) It wouldn't be a public protest about the Arabs being let down at Versailles?

GROUP CAPTAIN No. Asked him that.

FLIGHT LIEUTENANT Or the Palestine Question?

GROUP CAPTAIN No. Welcomes a Jewish State. (*He takes*

out a piece of paper) He fought for—er—yes, here it is. (*Reading*) He fought for the whole Semitic race, irrespective of religion. He has no grievance at all about either Arabia or Palestine. "Churchill's recent settlement of the Middle East has brought us out with clean hands." Those were his exact words.

FLIGHT LIEUTENANT Really? His exact words?

GROUP CAPTAIN (*Glowering*) Yes, but don't you quote them.

FLIGHT LIEUTENANT No, sir.

GROUP CAPTAIN Queer little fellow. If he wasn't who he is, you might feel quite sorry for him.

FLIGHT LIEUTENANT What's going to happen to him?

GROUP CAPTAIN Air Ministry are turning him out pronto. They're flaming mad. They're being badgered already by foreign embassies. Going to be questions in the House too. Oh no. I mean, you can't have the Service turned into a rest home for war heroes. Army too.

FLIGHT LIEUTENANT Legally *can* they turf him out?

GROUP CAPTAIN Oh yes. Entered under false name and false particulars.
(*There is a knock on the door*)

FLIGHT LIEUTENANT Come in.
(*The* FLIGHT SERGEANT *comes in and salutes*)

FLIGHT SERGEANT Flight Sergeant Thompson, B Flight, reporting, sir.

GROUP CAPTAIN Yes, Flight. It's about a man in your Flight. Aircraftman Ross.

FLIGHT SERGEANT Yes, sir.

GROUP CAPTAIN He has to be off this station within an hour.

FLIGHT SERGEANT Yes, sir.

GROUP CAPTAIN You knew about it?

FLIGHT SERGEANT He told me, sir.

GROUP CAPTAIN Did he tell you why?

FLIGHT SERGEANT Yes, sir.

GROUP CAPTAIN Oh, well, don't tell the rest of the Flight.

FLIGHT SERGEANT They all know, sir. I told them.

GROUP CAPTAIN Oh God! (*To* FLIGHT LIEUTENANT) It'll be all round the camp by now—

FLIGHT LIEUTENANT (*To* FLIGHT SERGEANT, *curiously*) Exactly what did he tell you, Flight?

FLIGHT SERGEANT What the Group Captain said to him,

sir. That he was the wrong type for the R.A.F. Didn't fit in. Was too old. Couldn't do the job—so he was being hoof—discharged the Service.
(*A pause*)

FLIGHT LIEUTENANT That's all he told you, Flight?

FLIGHT SERGEANT Yes, sir.

GROUP CAPTAIN Nothing else at all?

FLIGHT SERGEANT (*Trying to remember*) No, sir. Except that he didn't know—what he was going to do with himself now.

GROUP CAPTAIN That's all right, Flight. (*Dismissing him*) Thank you.

FLIGHT SERGEANT Leave to speak, sir. (*The* GROUP CAPTAIN *nods*) I've known this airman ten weeks. He's not an ideal recruit, but then who is? In fact he's not a bad little — (*He bites the word off*) chap at all. I think—if you only let him stay, sir—I can see to it that he won't get into no more trouble. And I'm sure, some day, he'll make an airman.
(*A pause*)

GROUP CAPTAIN I'm sorry, Flight—but it's all settled.

FLIGHT LIEUTENANT (*With a faint smile*) He doesn't fit in.

FLIGHT SERGEANT Yes, sir. It's just that it takes all sorts, sir —that's what I always say—

GROUP CAPTAIN (*Sharply*) That's enough, Flight. See that he's off the station by nine hundred hours—

FLIGHT SERGEANT Yes, sir. (*He salutes, marches to the door and turns*) Forgive forthrightness, sir. It's just I don't believe there's anyone in this world who can't be made to fit in somehow—

GROUP CAPTAIN Yes, Flight. Thank you.

FLIGHT SERGEANT Trust I have given no offense.

GROUP CAPTAIN No offense. It's just that Ross happens to be a special case. (*To* FLIGHT LIEUTENANT) A very special case.

FLIGHT SERGEANT Yes, sir.

(*He salutes and goes. The lights fade*)

SCENE EIGHT

Scene: Hut fourteen. LAWRENCE, *in civilian clothes, is packing a kitbag. He is looking out of the window, whence we hear the sound of a bugle. When it stops he turns back to his task.* NOLAN *comes in.*

NOLAN (*Embarrassed, but with false joviality*) Hullo, Rossie, boy. How's the world?

LAWRENCE All right. Break on?

NOLAN Yes.

LAWRENCE No cocoa and biscuits this morning?

NOLAN Not hungry. Rossie—
(*He holds out some money*)

LAWRENCE No. You keep that.

NOLAN Oh, but I couldn't. (*He puts the money on the bed*) You'll be needing it more than me now, anyway.

LAWRENCE (*Realizing resistance is useless*) Thank you, Paddy. I must give you back the half crown.

NOLAN (*As* LAWRENCE *holds it out*) Keep it, man. No,

keep it. It's not much, but it could help out there. What are you going to do?

LAWRENCE (*Putting the money away*) No idea, Paddy.

NOLAN Got a job to go to?

LAWRENCE No.

NOLAN It's terrible this unemployment. Terrible. I wouldn't be in this place if it weren't for that, I can tell you. No fear. You got a girl?

LAWRENCE No.

NOLAN (*Smiling*) Lucky man.

LAWRENCE Yes. I suppose so.

NOLAN One comfort—you don't have to tell her you got hoofed. Anyone to tell?

LAWRENCE No.

NOLAN I'll write to anyone if you'll give me the address. Say what bad luck it was you got on the wrong side of the Station Commander. Just unreasonable, I'll say he was— (PARSONS *comes in quickly*)

PARSONS Listen—I don't want no noes about this, because I've talked to all the others—except Paddy here and he'll say yes like the rest, I know—won't you, Paddy?

NOLAN (*Plaintively*) I don't know what it is, yet.

PARSONS (*Snarling*) I'm telling you, aren't I?

NOLAN Sorry.

PARSONS We're writing a document—quite dignified—most respectful—dear sir—we have the honor—all that cock—and we're all signing it and sending it to the Group Captain—and what we're going to say is that we all think that the way they're treating you is the most dirtiest, bleedingest trick that even those bastards have ever pulled on one of us—and that's saying something.

LAWRENCE (*Quietly*) On one of us?

PARSONS Yes—of course—but what I said just now—we must make it respectful—B Flight suggest there has been some slight misapprehension regarding Airman Ross not fitting in (*Warming to his subject*) because if he can fit into B Flight he can bloody-well fit into the R.A.F. or into any other bloody Service you can bloody-well think of—sir. (*Thoughtfully*) Trouble is, we're really going to need you to write this for us. Got the time?

LAWRENCE No. Besides you mustn't send it.

PARSONS Don't worry. We're sending it. Aren't we, Paddy?

NOLAN I'm game—if all the others are. Are they really, Sailor?

PARSONS (*Fiercely*) What kind of a mug do you think I am? In this sort of lark it's all or no one—see. One single blackleg—just one, and they'll beat us. There aren't no blacklegs on this.

LAWRENCE Dickinson?

PARSONS He's in. Thinks it's a joke, mind you, hasn't got no proper social conscience—officer class, you see—but he's in all right and glad to be. So you're in too, Paddy—right?

NOLAN Right.

PARSONS (*To* LAWRENCE) That's all of us, chum. So it's settled—

LAWRENCE (*Shaking his head, gently*) No.

PARSONS Why not?

LAWRENCE It can only mean trouble.

PARSONS (*Contemptuously*) Nah. What can they do? Hoof the whole Flight and have the papers talk about a mutiny at Uxbridge? Put us all on jankers, and have the story round the whole camp. No. Worst they'll do is collective reprimand. (*In his "officer" voice*) "None of you understand Service ways, my boys. That's your trouble." (*He makes a face*) *Best* they can do is reconsider—

LAWRENCE They won't do that.

PARSONS (*Obviously agreeing*) Well, it's a chance. There's always a chance, as the bishop said to the housemaid.

LAWRENCE Don't send it until tomorrow.

PARSONS Well—we thought—the sooner the better—

LAWRENCE No. Not until tomorrow.

PARSONS All right. Well, goodbye, Rossie.

LAWRENCE (*Taking his outstretched hand*) Goodbye, Sailor.

PARSONS (*Muttering*) The bastards! I could bloody-well murder them—I could go up to each and every one of them and collectively or individually screw all their—
(*He has disappeared.* NOLAN *also puts his hand out*)

NOLAN Goodbye, Rossie.

LAWRENCE Goodbye, Paddy.

NOLAN Good luck for the future.

LAWRENCE Thank you. The same to you. And thank you for the (*Remembering the slang*) half-dollar.
(NOLAN *makes a deprecating gesture and is going out as the* FLIGHT SERGEANT *comes in*)

FLIGHT SERGEANT What do you think you're doing, young Nolan? Think the break lasts all morning?

NOLAN I was talking to Ross.

FLIGHT SERGEANT *(Roaring)* I don't care if you were talking to the Aga Khan, get back on fatigue—

NOLAN Yes, Flight. Sorry, Flight—
(He flees. The FLIGHT SERGEANT *comes up to* LAWRENCE*)*

FLIGHT SERGEANT Ready, boy?

LAWRENCE Nearly.
(He turns to collect some books. The FLIGHT SERGEANT, *sitting on the bed, pulls out of the nearly filled kitbag* LAWRENCE'S *ornamental dagger)*

FLIGHT SERGEANT What's this?

LAWRENCE *(Carelessly)* Oh—sort of keepsake. Would you like to have it?

FLIGHT SERGEANT Well, thanks. I'll give it to the wife to hang on the wall. She loves stuff like that. I'm telling you, son, you'd have made an airman if the bleeders had only let you be. I told 'em that just now—head bleeder and all.

LAWRENCE Thank you, Flight. I'm grateful.

FLIGHT SERGEANT Didn't work, though. They got it in for you, proper, son—don't know why. Something to do with your past, shouldn't wonder.

LAWRENCE Yes. It may be.

FLIGHT SERGEANT Well, listen here, my boy, don't let them

get you down. What's past is past, see, and finished and dead. What you got to think about is the future. (*Looking at his watch*) Well—are you ready now?

LAWRENCE (*Pulling his kitbag closed and tying it*) Just about.

FLIGHT SERGEANT What are you going to do? Any idea?

LAWRENCE (*Head bent over kitbag*) Yes. I think I have. I'm going to get back into the R.A.F. as soon as I can.

FLIGHT SERGEANT (*Surprised*) Think you can do that?

LAWRENCE Well, I'll have to change my name, I suppose. Ross won't do any more. (*He points to the name "Ross" painted on his kitbag*) Shaw. I thought of that this morning. How do you like it?

FLIGHT SERGEANT All right.

LAWRENCE But it's not the name that matters. It's the number.

FLIGHT SERGEANT (*Wonderingly*) The number? What number?

LAWRENCE Oh, any number. Just provided it's one of a lot of others—like this.
(*He points to the number on his kitbag*)

FLIGHT SERGEANT I don't know what you're talking about. Do you really want another dose of all this?
(*He indicates the hut*)

LAWRENCE More than anything else I can think of.

FLIGHT SERGEANT You're a glutton for punishment, aren't you?

LAWRENCE (*Smiling*) It rather looks like it.

FLIGHT SERGEANT I've got to sneak you out through the Group Captain's private entrance. Gawd knows why. I'll get the key. You know his house? (LAWRENCE *nods*) I'll meet you over there.
(*He goes out.* LAWRENCE *finishes tying his kitbag, his head bent over it*)

LAWRENCE God will give you peace.
(*He looks round the hut for the last time and then, shouldering his kitbag, he follows the* FLIGHT SERGEANT *out. A distant bugle call is sounding as the curtain falls*)